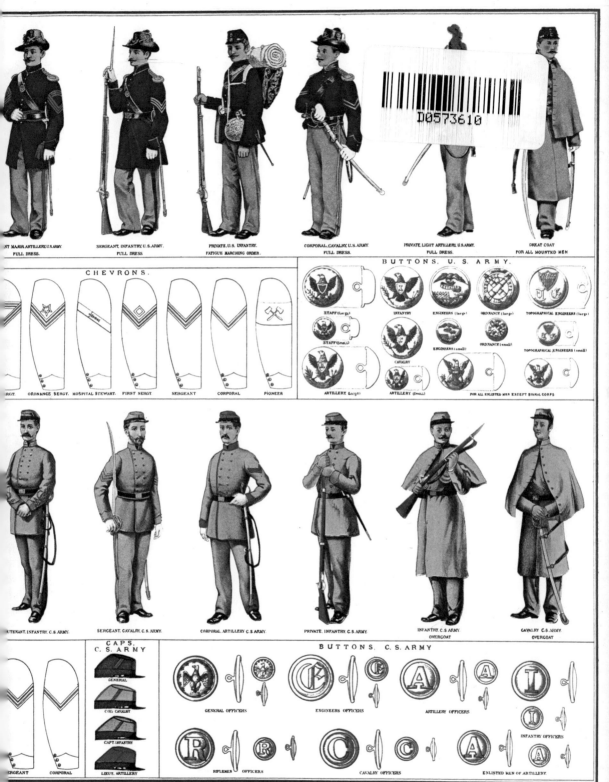

BUTTONS. U. S. ARMY.

CHEVRONS.

CAPS. C. S. ARMY

BUTTONS. C. S. ARMY

ATLAS TO ACCOMPANY THE OFFICIAL RECORDS OF THE UNION AND CONFEDERATE ARMIES, 1861–1865

THE CIVIL WAR

By Robert Paul Jordan, *National Geographic Assistant Editor*

Produced by the National Geographic Special Publications Division
Robert L. Breeden, *Chief*

National Geographic Society
Melvin M. Payne, *President*
Melville Bell Grosvenor, *Editor-in-Chief*
Gilbert M. Grosvenor, *Editor*

THE CIVIL WAR

By ROBERT PAUL JORDAN
National Geographic Senior Assistant Editor

Published by
THE NATIONAL GEOGRAPHIC SOCIETY

MELVIN M. PAYNE, *President*
MELVILLE BELL GROSVENOR, *Editor-in-Chief*
GILBERT M. GROSVENOR, *Editor*
HOWELL WALKER, *Consulting Editor*
  for this book

Prepared by
THE SPECIAL PUBLICATIONS DIVISION

ROBERT L. BREEDEN, *Editor*
DONALD J. CRUMP, *Manuscript Editor*
MARY ANN HARRELL, *Assistant to the Editor*
MARGERY G. DUNN, TADD FISHER, MARY
  ANN HARRELL, TEE LOFTIN SNELL,
  PENELOPE W. SPRINGER, PEGGY D.
  WINSTON, *Research*
RICHARD M. CRUM, RONALD M. FISHER,
  TADD FISHER, MARY ANN HARRELL,
  H. ROBERT MORRISON, *Picture Legends*
DOROTHY M. CORSON, VIRGINIA THOMPSON,
  Index
JUDITH C. FORD, CAROL R. TEACHEY,
  SANDRA A. TURNER, BARBARA J.
  WALKER, *Editorial Assistants*
DR. JAY LUVAAS, *Consultant*
  Professor of History, Allegheny College

Illustrations

DAVID R. BRIDGE, *Picture Editor*
GERALDINE LINDER, TEE LOFTIN SNELL,
  BETTY STRAUSS, PEGGY D. WINSTON,
  Picture Research

Art Direction

JOSEPH A. TANEY, *Art Director*
JOSEPHINE B. BOLT, *Assistant Art Director*
RICHARD SCHLECHT, *Paintings and inset
  maps, pages 88-89, 102-103, 106-107,
  123, 130-131, 138-139, 159*

VIRGINIA L. BAZA, BOBBY G. CROCKETT,
  JOHN D. GARST, JR., *Map Research and
  Production, pages 24, 92*

Production and Printing

ROBERT W. MESSER, *Production Manager*
ANN H. CROUCH, JUDY L. STRONG,
  Production Assistants

JAMES R. WHITNEY, JOHN R. METCALFE,
  Engraving and Printing

Third Printing 1975

*Stillness pervades Virginia's Fredericksburg Na-
tional Cemetery, solemn reminder of the Civil War
and 600,000 Americans who fell like the leaves
of autumn. Title page: Union soldiers rally round
the flag—symbol of the lofty cause that triggered
four years of hatred and strife. Page 1: His genera-
tion sacrificed to war, 16-year-old Georgia private
Edwin Francis Jemison—killed at Malvern Hill,
Virginia—haunts the conscience of a new century.*

FOREWORD

On a muggy July night in 1862 a brigade bugler sounded "lights out" and quiet settled over a Union encampment beside the muddy James River. Calls of other buglers in distant units drifted over the Virginia countryside, melting into the stillness.

A Union general, Daniel Butterfield, watched from his tent as darkness swallowed the flames of candles and cooking fires. As the last sharp notes of the bugle had sounded, they seemed harsh to him and inappropriate for the hushed mood at day's end. Soon afterward Butterfield summoned his bugler and told him he wanted a new, more fitting call. Moreover, he would compose it!

Butterfield began to whistle; the bugler played, finally writing the melody on an envelope. Then he substituted it for the official version. It caught on. Other buglers copied it, and some carried it to distant fields of battle. Today we know that call as Taps, part of a legacy from a century past and from a war that split our Nation.

In this book Robert Paul Jordan reveals much of that legacy, taking us from the bitter prewar disputes over principles to the armed clashes over battlegrounds. Beginning at his Maryland home, not far from Manassas and Gettysburg, Bob traveled with his family—as others of us may wish to do after reading this book—to study well-known major battlefields, now serene and parklike. He also went to many of those hardly remembered, some of them swampy and overgrown with brush, just as they were when Rebels and Yankees tore through brier patches and thickets—and at each other.

With candor Bob Jordan strips away the romanticism so often associated with the war and exaggerated with time, bringing us up quickly to the reality of it all: the anguish of President Lincoln searching for a general who would fight, the gnawing hunger of a shivering and shoeless Confederate soldier, the fear in once-proud cities besieged and bombarded for weeks.

We see the tenacious U. S. Grant, capable of demanding unconditional surrender and of giving such generous surrender terms at Appomattox that history ranks him one of the most magnanimous men of the war. We stand near a somber Robert E. Lee as he struggles in his great personal dilemma, finally affirming with deep sorrow that duty calls him to his state and ultimately to the South. We watch him emerge the most revered losing general in history. We meet the lesser-known, but equally noble in spirit: Union Pvt. Leonidas Jordan, the author's great-uncle, who wrote his mother: "...if I ever geet home again I will apriciate religious things more"; and Rebel Sgt. Richard Kirkland, who risked enemy fire at the Battle of Fredericksburg to carry water to the dying Yankees whose screams he could no longer bear.

Such intimate glimpses into the lives of the men who fought the war pervade this book—experiences we share through letters, paintings, photographs, diaries, and newspapers of the day—all brought together in this story of the great national tragedy that Lincoln's Secretary of State once called the "irrepressible conflict."

ROBERT L. BREEDEN, *Editor*

CONTENTS

Union scout, a far-ranging observer for his unit, halts his lathered steed
on a dusty country lane and searches the distance for signs of the enemy.

GILBERT GAUL, M. KNOEDLER & COMPANY, NEW YORK CITY

Walker. 1888.

1820-1860:
THE YEARS OF COMPROMISE

CHAPTER ONE

ABRUPTLY THE SOFT MONOTONE pitched to high urgency in the earphones, fading and rising like a distant siren as Ken Parks swept his mine detector back and forth. He poised it where the signal echoed strongest. "Dig there," he directed his 12-year-old son and namesake, an old hand at these expeditions. Eagerly my own son, Robert, broke in— "Could I do it, please?" Young Ken graciously offered him the pick, and Robbie energetically began chopping the sticky Mississippi loam.

All city boys should enjoy such good luck, I thought. Clutching vines had tripped him, briers raked his face; he was cold, wet, and muddy— and he dug away happily oblivious to all. My 11-year-old lad hoped to unearth some relic of the Civil War; a shell fragment, perhaps, or a bullet, or even a bayonet.

What better place to search? This great battlefield lay unmarked and forgotten, though just north of us cars and trucks raced over the new superhighway between Jackson, Mississippi's capital, and Vicksburg. To me, the land seemed haunted in the pale winter sun, an eerie mélange of brush-snarled ravines and wooded ridges running to a commanding promontory, Champion Hill. Nearly 7,000 soldiers of North and South fell on this soil in a few hours in the crucial battle of the decisive campaign in the West. But time hangs motionless now over Champion Hill, and many another fallow field of combat. The elements work little change; it is memory the years blur.

Walking over such battlegrounds in the company of experts, you can bridge the century and see the conflict come alive. Ken Parks—a film producer based in Jackson and one of many Civil War students to whom I am indebted—literally brooms the path of Ulysses S. Grant's Vicksburg campaign with his mine detector. His trained eye pinpoints the fiercest fighting by the volume of the metal he unearths, and history touches today.

Suddenly Robbie linked past to present in his own fashion. "Here it is!" he yelled. Three inches deep he had grubbed up a Minié ball, a bullet undisturbed since May 16, 1863. I turned it in my fingers. The conical lead slug bore no rifling grooves, no flattening signs of impact. It had never been fired. It was a "drop."

In mind's eye the drama flashed before me: All about, I see Union soldiers crouching in the shelter of this gully, waiting to resume the attack. Hot, thirsty troops, some of them boys in their early teens, pull at up-tilted canteens; rivulets of sweat streak powder-blackened faces. At my side, an infantryman draws his ramrod and fumbles in the cartridge box on his hip. A Minié ball drops unnoticed from it to the earth while he rams another down his muzzle-loading rifle-musket.

Worn-out field hands symbolize the institution of bondage that by the mid-1800's had cut deep and increasingly bitter divisions between the South and the rest of the Nation. By 1860 the need to resolve the inflammatory issue had become unmistakably more urgent—and far more difficult.

Henry Clay of Kentucky pleads for compromise before a somber Senate as a crisis of disunion racks the Nation in 1850. Southerners demand as a right the free-dom to take slaves into western land recently acquired from Mexico; free-soil leaders oppose them; the rancor of this dispute spreads to other issues. Next to Vice President Millard Fillmore (presiding), John C. Calhoun of South Carolina listens grimly. Mortally ill, he will reply that compromise betrays the South—if need be she will secede "and part in peace." Daniel Webster, head in hand, will speak for the Union above all, with a stronger fugitive slave law to placate the Southern states. But William H. Seward, seated at extreme left, will warn that God's opposition to slavery's expansion is "a higher law than the Constitution." The Compromise of 1850 resulted. It gave only an interval of harmony, and left the clash of principles unresolved. As the decade passed, new crises arose.

These Yankees soon scrambled up and over the gully and moved down the other side, into a vicious hail of Rebel lead. So did we, and I shuddered at the murderousness of it 105 years later as Ken's mine detector led us to ball after ball. Many were mashed almost flat. Fired at 50-foot range, they impacted against the Union onslaught with crushing force.

The Battle of Champion Hill raged from midmorning to late afternoon. Some terrain was fought over three times. "What was it really like?" Robbie asked.

I told him about the Confederate colonel who galloped along his brigade's lines, a knight-errant of old. He clutched the reins and a large magnolia flower in one hand while waving his sword with the other. "Charge!" he cried, and charge his men did.

I read my son the words of a terrified Federal corporal who had run for his life: "It was terribly hot . . . and an enemy on flank and rear shouting and firing. The grass, the stones, the bushes, seemed melting under the shower of bullets that was following us to the rear. . . . Like ten thousand starving and howling wolves the enemy pursued. . . ."

And I recalled the little mound of pine boughs heaped on a grassy knoll we had visited earlier. Newly placed, they marked the shallow grave of an unknown Confederate, buried where death caught him and discovered by chance only recently. The soldier's uniform had turned to dust; its metal buttons remained, resting in perfect alignment.

In the end the Federals prevailed at Champion Hill. After this crucial defeat the Rebels chose to retreat into Fortress Vicksburg, 20 miles west on bluffs above the Mississippi River. Starvation siege followed. Inevitably the citadel surrendered, severing the rebellious states to the west. Now the North would crack the South into smaller bits, although nearly two more years of agony must elapse before the task was finished.

What caused the Civil War? Why did Americans fight one another four long years, at a cost of more than 600,000 lives? What did it all mean? What does it signify today?

I sought out scholars, both in books and on the scene, and they supplied a multitude of answers. They agreed on no overriding cause, only that slavery and secession lay at the crux.

How odd, then, to realize that not one Southerner in ten owned slaves—the census of 1860 listed just 383,637 slaveowners out of 1,516,000 families. Many had misgivings about the "peculiar institution," as they called it. In fact, up to 1830 the South led the country in efforts to achieve gradual emancipation or recolonize Negroes in Africa. As for secession, probably only a scant majority at most ever favored disunion before the final crisis.

Incongruities like these beset Civil War students at every turn. Northerners wore Rebel gray, Southerners donned the Federal blue. At the siege of Vicksburg, Missouri supplied the Union with 22 units and the South with 17. Pro-Union men held firm all through the war in the Appalachian country of western North Carolina, eastern Tennessee, and farther south; a cavalry company of white Alabamians rode with Sherman on his march to the sea. Virginia's western counties, with old grudges against the tidewater planters, seceded from the rest of the state, and in 1863 joined the Union as West Virginia.

Several of Abraham Lincoln's in-laws served with the South, one as a general. Former President John Tyler, a Virginian, won a seat in the Confederate House of Representatives. Robert E. Lee, the South's magnificent fighting leader, thought slavery evil and secession unjustified. The North's indomitable Ulysses S. Grant owned a slave before the war; hard up for money, he might have sold William Jones for $1,000, but chose to set him free.

On and on runs the catalogue of anomalies. I have found at least thirty different names for the conflict—a fair measure of how differently people viewed it. The variety even in brief proves startling: the War Against Northern Aggression, the War for States' Rights, the War for Constitutional Liberty, the War for the Preservation of the Union, the Brothers' War, Mr. Lincoln's War. Southerners preferred to speak of "our second War of Independence."

Some Southerners today eschew calling it the Civil War, preferring the War Between the States. The U. S. Official Records use "the War of the Rebellion." No matter the nomenclature. The struggle remains our most momentous national experience, and its vitality still stirs our land. In retracing the complex ordeal, I soon determined that its full significance eludes us, for an excellent reason. The results continue to come in, most notably in the field of civil rights.

My wife Jane and our three children accompanied me whenever school holidays permitted. We are a fortunate family. Much of our country's great story unfolds close to our home in Bethesda, Maryland, near the Nation's Capital. The Civil War, especially, beckons on every hand. We drive north to Gettysburg in an hour or so, and find it almost incredible that more than 170,000 Americans tried to kill one another among these serene Pennsylvania fields and orchards, hills and vales. Sometimes we drive northwest to Harper's Ferry, within easy range in West Virginia where the Shenandoah and Potomac Rivers marry. I always feel a sense of melancholy when the old town looms up, as if the fanatical abolitionist John Brown, his attempt at a slave insurrection a failure, had imposed one last and abiding remonstrance.

From our garden we look south across the Potomac into Virginia— tragic Virginia just over a century ago, epicenter of the war. About 22 percent of the fighting occurred on Old Dominion soil. We journey rapidly to Fredericksburg, Richmond, Petersburg, Appomattox, and marvel at the deeds they have seen. Not far from us flows Bull Run; we know where forgotten earthworks line the silent stream—trenches still well-defined, dug by Southerners before the battle and strengthened in the first winter of the war to protect their lines near the "old Capital."

Even modern Washington, world crossroads, readily yields up evidence of Civil War days. A sleepy Southern city of 61,000 in 1860, it rapidly became a threshing armed camp, replete with spies and full of panic when Confederate legions approached. President Lincoln himself faced Rebel bullets at Fort Stevens, where restored ramparts stand today not five miles from the White House.

"Get down, you damned fool, before you get shot!" bawled a youthful captain below the parapet, and Lincoln got down unruffled and unharmed, the only President ever to undergo enemy fire. Oliver Wendell Holmes, Jr., a future Associate Justice of the United States Supreme Court, had warned a civilian—and then recognized him.

Harriet Beecher Stowe of New England shook the conscience of millions with Uncle Tom's Cabin, *published in 1852. Her famous book gained immediate success in spite of attempts to suppress it in the South. The first American novel with a black hero, it stirred a deep new sympathy for the slave.*

Dred Scott, perhaps the most famous American slave, lost a legal bid for liberty but his case fired passions to put an end to bondage. His lawsuit claimed that residence on free soil made him a free man. The Supreme Court said no, leaving him in terms of law an "ordinary article of merchandise." More important, the Court held that Congress had no power to limit the expansion of slavery. In response, citizens joining the new Republican Party resolved to see this decision changed.

Civil War America surrounds us, but we see it differently. At the outset, our 7-year-old daughter Meredith tried to distinguish "good guys" from bad. Jane and I gently dissuaded her. My wife's forebears rode out of Kentucky for the Confederacy with Morgan's Raiders. Mine marched from Ohio in Union ranks. Meredith did find a hero, though. After she painstakingly read the Gettysburg Address in the national cemetery where it was delivered, Lincoln became her man.

Geography briefly troubled Julia, our inquisitive 5-year-old. When I departed for St. Albans, Vermont, where a score of young Kentuckians plundered three banks in the war's northernmost land action, she asked if I were leaving the country.

Not quite, I replied. St. Albans sits 15 miles below the Canadian border, across which the raiding Southerners fled on horseback to sanctuary. But Georgia once *did* fervently desire Vermont to leave the country, thundering that "...a ditch should be dug around Vermont and the pestiferous State be floated out to sea."

You and I, looking on with history's perspective, may smile. Georgia, however, intended anything but levity. Wroth over Vermont's vehement antislavery sentiment, she was only expressing her side, and the South's, of an increasingly bitter debate. Firebrands of both sections for decades broadcast abuse on politics, economics, and morals until reason no longer could be heard. Dissension finally erupted in disaster at Fort Sumter, South Carolina, on April 12, 1861, although shots had been fired months earlier elsewhere.

Negro slavery existed in all the colonies long before the American Revolution. It proved unprofitable in the North and failed to flourish; climate, one-man farms, growing industrialism, urbanization, immigration, the small number of resident Negroes, and conscience all militated against it. Legal measures—statutes, constitutions, court decisions—provided for gradual emancipation and abolition. In 1775 Rhode Island gave freedom to any child born of a slave mother. Vermont took action in 1777. In 1787 the Northwest Ordinance barred slavery from the lands north of the Ohio River and east of the Mississippi. New York provided for gradual abolition in 1799; in 1817 she passed a law to end all slavery within her borders on July 4, 1827. The Federal Government had forbidden importation of Negroes after January 1, 1808.

WHILE THE NORTH found its future in the factory, the Southern states clung to their pastoral way of life. Living by agriculture, they depended on slave labor to produce much of the rice, sugar, tobacco, corn, indigo, wheat, and cotton—cotton above all. It became extremely profitable after the cotton gin's invention in 1793; as the Gulf states developed, new cotton fields multiplied. The demand for field hands soared commensurately; the zeal for emancipation ebbed, replaced by fear.

Horror and dread flared through the South in August 1831, with the news of Nat Turner's rebellion. In the role of a prophet, Turner led some 70 fellow slaves against the whites around them in Southampton County, Virginia. About 57 white people, many of them women and children, died before the revolt was crushed in blood. In the months that followed, the Virginia legislature argued out the South's last public debate on slavery, and voted to keep the *Continued on page 18*

13

EYRE CROWE, C. 1859 (ABOVE), AND HERMANN HERZOG, COURTESY JAY P. ALTMAYER

"Fine lot of slaves up for sale, men, women, and children — not sold for any fault — jist to settle an estate." Street cries like this called customers to the slave traders to select a likely servant or two. Humane owners tried to avoid splitting up a family, but a husband might cling helplessly to his wife's hand while the auctioneer's chant elicited the bid that would separate them for life. When Eyre Crowe of England sketched such scenes in Richmond in 1853, suspicious and angry dealers made him leave the market. Plantation slaves lived in crude cabins with the barest necessities, a little distance from the owner's residence.

Harper's Ferry wakes to early morning as a freight train rumbles across the Potomac River, westward bound; at the foot of the Blue Ridge Mountains, the Shenandoah River (left) rushes down from the Valley of Virginia. Visitors

Harper's Ferry enjoys its last peace before armies fight to control the Baltimore & Ohio, all-important rail link to the West, and march north to outflank Washington or south to plunder the fertile Valley. Here, in 1861, Rebels took arms machinery and 5,000 muskets from Arsenal stores. In 1859, John Brown with 21 raiders tried vainly to seize guns and raise a slave revolt. The South, frightened and furious, saw Brown as a murderous agent of abolition; many Northerners hailed him as a martyr.

to the little town today can see the armory fire-engine house where Col. Robert E. Lee cornered insurrectionist John Brown and his followers in 1859; nearby rests the foundation of the old Arsenal, burned by the Federals in 1861.

DAVID R. BRIDGE, NATIONAL GEOGRAPHIC STAFF

peculiar institution. Thereafter, more and more Southerners closed their minds to any argument for emancipation; yet they could not escape an underlying fear that—by rebellion or individual murder—their property would strike them down. Fear of violence and reliance on force were inevitable, and ever-present.

For all of that, vast quantities of the great staple crops were raised on plantations, with human chattels manning the production line. In one sense planters ruled the Southland; they formed a wealthy and powerful aristocracy with fixed traditions and manners—a baronial way of life and cavalier philosophy that set a tone for the rest. Mountaineers, small farmers, professional men—all embraced one plantation ideal: They too considered themselves men of independence, monarchs of their own realm.

DIVERSE AS THE SOUTH WAS, here sprang its unity and its ardent nationalism. Whatever his lot, the white Southerner looked on life as his own master and gave a profound allegiance to his state, his section, his home. To him, only slaves—and the unhappy souls toiling for others in Northern factories—weren't free.

By 1860, four million Negroes lived in the eleven states that were to secede—a region occupied by only five and a half million whites. Slavery conditioned every aspect of daily life, fastening itself so firmly that the difficulty of ending the practice seemed insuperable. White Southerners feared that emancipation must create not only social but economic chaos; the vast capital investment in slaves underlay the South's entire economic structure. Prime field hands brought from $1,000 to $1,500 each at auction, sometimes more.

The blunt print of an old handbill conveyed a poignant awareness of servitude to Jane and me one day at the Old Slave Mart Museum in Charleston, South Carolina. We stopped before a framed auction notice and studied it together:

"List of an Uncommonly Prime and Orderly Gang of 89 Negroes. Accustomed to the Culture of Rice, Cotton, and Provisions. Will be sold at auction Monday the Sixth Day of February 1860 at 11 o'clock A.M. One-third cash, balance payable in one, two, three years."

Buyers bid on slaves by number, consecutively. No. 1 on this list was Grace, age 50, a "full hand." This meant that Grace would accomplish the daily "task" assigned to her—a workload predicated on what the slowest slave could perform in eight hours, not counting an hour for the noon meal. When the auctioneer came to No. 9, Martha, age 25, on the list, prospective buyers noted different qualifications: "Cripple, good breeder."

So the list ran—89 black humans, some of them children and infants, for sale to the highest bidder. "I can understand the abolitionists' fervor," said Jane.

Still, it wasn't necessary to be an abolitionist *Continued on page 27*

John Brown's spirit—gun in one hand, Bible in the other—strides above war dead in this allegory of conflict. Slaves look to him in desperate hope as their masters go into battle. In the van of Union forces, leaders of abolition stand on guard: the sage with his book, the free-soil settler of Kansas with his rifle.

JOHN STEUART CURRY, 1941, KANSAS STATE CAPITOL

Abraham Lincoln, who would lead the Union through four years of Civil War, tried his hand at several ways to make a living in the small settlement at New Salem, Illinois (right), before moving on to Springfield, the state capital. There he be-

Friends and neighbors honor t

Republican Lincoln and Democrat Stephen A. Douglas, "the Little Giant," debate free-soil issues and Dred Scott's case in the Senate campaign of 1858. Lincoln lost this election, but won his party's nomination for President in 1860.

came a well-known, prosperous
lawyer and won election to the
Illinois legislature and to Congress. He earned wider recognition for his unequaled sense
of justice and for his clear
analysis of national issues,
notably the slavery dilemma.

NATIONAL GEOGRAPHIC PHOTOGRAPHER JAMES L. STANFIELD

andidate at his Springfield home in August 1860; in November they celebrated his election to the Presidency.

COURTESY CHICAGO HISTORICAL SOCIETY

Doffing his hat in salute to the crowd, Abraham Lincoln rides up Pennsylvania Avenue to his inauguration on March 4, 1861, with President James Buchanan at his side. A reporter called Lincoln "pale and composed" in the shadow of the

new Confederacy. For the first time in American history, a President took office as
the leader of a purely sectional party; ten slave states kept his name off the ballot.
In his Inaugural Address he pleaded for unity: "We must not be enemies," he said.

Jefferson Davis (left) takes office as provisional President of the Confederacy (opposite) to lead the states that seceded at the news of Lincoln's election. By him stands Howell Cobb of Georgia (below), who presided over the organization of an interim government in 1861. A reporter noted solemnity of "almost unnatural grandeur" at the ceremony in the portico of the state capitol in Montgomery, Alabama, February 18; Davis declared, "... our true policy is peace. ..." The map below shows how war divided the states.

THE NATION IN 1861

Union states
Confederate states
Border states
Statehood 1863
Territories

Prewar Richmond, tranquil and prosperous, crowns riverside hills above the Kanawha Canal at the head of navigation on the James River. Her famous Tredegar Iron Works provided ordnance for Southern forces throughout the conflict. At her white-columned state capitol, serving the new national government, Davis became President under a permanent Constitution on February 22, 1862. He and his wife Varina (right) greet officers and their ladies attending a formal reception at "the White House of the Confederacy."

LITHOGRAPH, 1834, AFTER GEORGE COOKE (BELOW), AND W. L. SHEPPARD, VALENTINE MUSEUM, RICHMOND

to detest slavery. Abraham Lincoln, in 1854, denounced mere indifference to the spread of slavery, because of "the monstrous injustice of slavery itself. I hate it because . . . it enables the enemies of our free institutions, with plausibility, to taunt us as hypocrites—causes the real friends of freedom to doubt our sincerity, and especially because it forces so many good men amongst ourselves into an open war with the very fundamental principles of civil liberty. . . ."

But Lincoln did not denounce the holders of slaves. "I surely will not blame them," he said, "for not doing what I should not know how to do myself. If all earthly power were given to me, I should not know what to do, as to the existing institution."

The answer, he believed, needed time. He also believed, passionately, that the Union must be preserved. " 'A house divided against itself cannot stand,' " said the future President. "I believe this government cannot endure, permanently half *slave* and half *free*. . . . It will become *all* one thing, or *all* the other."

Many men disagreed with the idea of one Nation indivisible, and some were Northerners. Emancipation now, clamored the abolitionists, or dissolve the Union. Strange words, perhaps, coming out of the North, with its growing belief in Federal sovereignty. Talk of disunion, however, was music to Southerners, who preached state's rights as a first principle. Both slavery and secession were matters for individual states to decide, they trumpeted, and neither was ruled out by the Constitution.

On the first point they were perfectly correct. As time passed and slavery came to seem a shameful remnant of the past to many Americans and to Europeans, Southerners clung to the letter of the Constitution as their defense for their "domestic institutions." On the second point they could not invoke a text beyond dispute; they turned, often, to the great precedent of the American Revolution as their fathers and grandfathers had known it. In defense of fundamental rights, a people might dissolve the political bands that linked them with another, declare their independence, and assume a separate and equal station among the powers of the earth, as Thomas Jefferson had said.

Years after the war, Jefferson Davis, the unreconstructed former President of the Confederate States of America, echoed in his apologia the basic premise of the Lost Cause. It still has a familiar ring:

"No alternative remained except to seek the security out of the Union which they had vainly tried to obtain within it. The hope of our people may be stated in a sentence. It was to escape from injury and strife in the Union, to find prosperity and peace out of it."

With this explanation in mind, my son and I spent considerable time discussing the events that led to war. Once I asked what he believed its one great cause might be.

He thought a moment. "Hate," Robbie said.

There was that, in abundance. But William   *Continued on page 32*

Overleaf: Ironworkers forge a shaft in the foundry at Cold Spring, New York. Thus in the North free men built the industrial might of the Union and produced its weapons. Late in 1860 William Tecumseh Sherman, weeping, warned a Southern friend: ". . . in all history no nation of mere agriculturalists ever made successful war against a nation of mechanics. . . . You are bound to fail."

J. F. WEIR, 1877, METROPOLITAN MUSEUM OF ART, GIFT OF LYMAN G. BLOOMINGDALE

The Cotton Kingdom: Field hands get in a crop on a Mississippi plantation; double-teamed mules drag bales to the steamboat waiting at a river landing (center). A rule of thumb tied the price of a workman to that of cotton; if cotton brought 12 cents a pound, a planter might pay $1,200 for a slave. Southern leaders relied on the demand for cotton in Britain and France to assure foreign intervention and a short war — if they actually had to fight. They did not foresee the fatal strain with which war would overload their railroad net, laid down haphazardly to serve their agriculture. The Union Depot in Atlanta, Georgia (right), serving four lines, had all too few equivalents within the Confederacy.

W. A. WALKER, 1881, COURTESY JAY P. ALTMAYER (ABOVE); WILBUR G. KURTZ, 1959, COURTESY W. G. RYCKMAN

H. Seward, Lincoln's Secretary of State, summed it up best, I think, in three words: "the irrepressible conflict." Perhaps war finally rent the land because it was ineluctable, because only a blood purge would shock the country into its senses. True, both sides tried to avert bloodshed. No measures availed for long, and some only heightened the tension. New developments fueled the antagonism in new ways.

In 1820, the Missouri Compromise prohibited slavery in lands of the Louisiana Purchase north of Missouri's southern border; and its provisions acquired almost the standing of the Constitution itself. Yet in 1832 the entire Nation grew tense as South Carolina adopted an ordinance nullifying Federal tariffs as measures that favored Northern manufacturers. The fiery state threatened secession. President Andrew Jackson promised a lower tariff—and issued a proclamation warning that "Disunion by armed force is *treason*." This crisis ebbed; the lower tariff of March 1833 placated the state.

In 1849, cries of disunion again resounded throughout the Southland. California wanted to enter the Union as a free state, which would destroy the Senate balance of 15 free and 15 slave states. Southerners would lose the political power they had enjoyed so many years. After long and bitter debate, the Compromise of 1850 emerged. California entered the Union as a free state; the South got a tougher fugitive-slave law as a sop. Another law defined the boundaries of Texas, which received $10 million for ceding her claims to land in New Mexico. Both New Mexico and Utah gained territorial status, with the right to decide the question of slavery on their soil. A fifth law forbade the slave trade in the District of Columbia.

This settlement brought a measure of calm to a distracted country, but it dealt with specific problems only. The conflict of principle remained. Was slavery a positive good? A necessary evil? An evil to be destroyed at any price? Not only a baffling problem in itself, it came to symbolize—and embitter—all sectional differences.

Robert P. Jordan, Jr., 11, son of the author, selects a toy artillery piece in the souvenir shop of the Old Slave Mart Museum in Charleston, South Carolina.

The author escorts his daughter Julia, 5, down high steps to the quadrangle of Charleston's Old Citadel building, which in the 1860's housed the South Carolina Military Academy and gave the college its present name—The Citadel. Cadets and alumni rallied to arms in the cause of Southern independence.

Then, in 1852, *Uncle Tom's Cabin,* Harriet Beecher Stowe's melodramatic novel about slavery's evils, roused emotions to new heights both North and South. It sold 5,000 copies in the first week of publication, more than 300,000 in the first year in the United States alone.

The drums of war boomed ever closer as the 1850's wore on, and the South increasingly felt itself on the defensive. In 1854, the Kansas-Nebraska Act wiped out the old Missouri Compromise line and opened more of the West to slavery. In swift response the young Republican Party dedicated itself to repeal of the law and to limits on the spread of slavery. The party grew, as Kansas flamed into anarchy. A pro-slavery posse of "border ruffians" sacked the town of Lawrence, and John Brown began his deadly crusade at Pottawatomie Creek. "Bleeding Kansas" deserved its grim sobriquet.

IN 1857, THE UNITED STATES Supreme Court enraged opponents of slavery throughout the North and West. Eleven years earlier, a Missouri Negro named Dred Scott had sued for his freedom. He had lived on free soil as established by the Missouri Compromise, and thus, he contended, he became a free man. The case finally worked its way to the top, and he lost it.

The Court held that Congress had no power to limit the expansion of slavery—the Missouri Compromise had always been unconstitutional. Therefore Scott remained a slave. Moreover, three Justices said that no Negro—member of an inferior race—could ever be a citizen of the United States.

Time began running out. At Harper's Ferry on October 16, 1859, fierce-eyed John Brown with 21 followers, white and black, captured the United States Arsenal. Alarm raced through the slave states, ever fearful of a Negro uprising.

Robert E. Lee, Colonel, United States Army, was dispatched by train from Washington to command a detachment of Marines. Start to finish, John Brown's invasion lasted 36 hours, ending when Lee captured him. Brown was tried for murder, fomenting slave insurrection, and treason against Virginia, convicted, and hanged. The antislavery North had a martyr; the South, a foreboding of horror.

An ominous sign appeared in April 1860. The only political party that embraced all sections, the "one and indivisible Democracy," met in Charleston, South Carolina, to choose a candidate for President. It split along sectional lines on the issue of slavery in the territories. Southern delegates walked out to name a man of their own; angry men from the North and West would choose Stephen A. Douglas.

The die was cast on November 6, 1860, with election of Abraham Lincoln, the Republican candidate, as President. He opposed slavery's spread, although he had no idea of interfering with its existing limits, and he stood foursquare for preservation of the Nation. His popularity in the slave states is reflected in the number of votes that ten of them gave him: exactly none. He couldn't get on the ballot.

North and South had reached the crossroads. The day after Lincoln's election, South Carolina hauled down the American flag at Charleston and raised its own ensign, the Palmetto flag. On December 20, she took the path leading out of the Union. The other cotton states quickly followed: Mississippi, Florida, Alabama, Georgia, Louisiana, and Texas.

But eight slave states still remained loyal, at least temporarily: Virginia, North Carolina, Arkansas, Tennessee, Delaware, Maryland, Kentucky, and Missouri. And many leaders of both sections did not think war need break out, though as a matter of state sovereignty Southerners had begun seizing United States property—forts, arsenals, navy yards, and the like—even before the Confederacy was formed. As armed instruments of a foreign and unfriendly power—the Union—these could not be tolerated by the secessionists.

Jefferson Davis, then a United States Senator from Mississippi, spoke of hope for peace. Sadly resigning his seat, he wished his confreres well, continuing, ". . . and such, I am sure, is the feeling of the people whom I represent toward those whom you represent. I, therefore, feel that I but express their desire when I say I hope, and they hope, for peaceable relations with you, though we must part."

I thought many times of the terrible irony in Davis's eloquent plea as I moved about the country. It came forcibly to mind one day while I lingered on the drawbridge at old Fort Barrancas, a crumbling stronghold long retired from duty and now surrounded by the U. S. Naval Air Station and sunny Pensacola, Florida.

On January 8, 1861—two weeks before Davis rose in the Senate to say farewell, and three months before cannon bombarded beleaguered Union troops at Fort Sumter, South Carolina—shots were fired here.

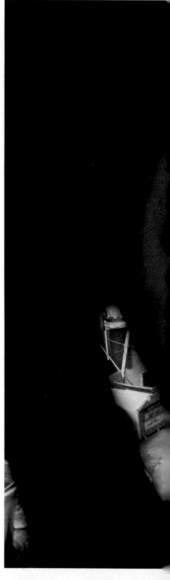

ALABAMA STATE TROOPS already had occupied nearby Forts Morgan and Gaines, Federal works guarding the entrance to Mobile Bay. Pensacola, with its naval and civilian shipyards and its railroad running to Montgomery, Alabama, offered an irresistible target. First Lt. Adam Slemmer, USA, acting commander at Fort Barrancas, posted guards to protect ammunition stores: Secessionists will not grab *this* Federal property, not if he can help it.

About midnight on January 8, a sentry's sharp challenge breaks the stillness. "Halt! Who goes there?" No answer. The soldier sounds the alarm and fires at shadowy figures lurking beyond the drawbridge. In the dark distance beats the drum's long roll, the call to arms. Federals leap from their bunks. The intruders break and run, footsteps resounding along the plank walk.

Yankee at work: Charles Hansen

That was all. For once the seizure of Government land and arms had been firmly resisted. Slemmer then moved his 46 soldiers and 30 sailors to more easily defensible Fort Pickens on the tip of alligator-ridden Santa Rosa Island in Pensacola Bay. Fort Pickens, and Fort Monroe on the Virginia Peninsula's tip, became the only important Federal installations in the South to remain in Union hands throughout the war.

A month later, the cotton states' delegates convened in Montgomery, Alabama. They formed the Confederate States of America, drafted an interim constitution, and chose Jefferson Davis as provisional President.

I gazed out absently from Fort Barrancas across Pensacola's placid harbor, taken suddenly by the appalling immensity of what lay ahead for North and South, shocked by the rebellious states' temerity and thrilled by their fortitude.

The South had farms, not factories. What chance did it have against

ishing expert, deftly strings a new drum near a model with red rim and strap, used by Federals in the Civil War.

At the Noble & Cooley factory (above) in Granville, Massachusetts, crafts-men turned out drums by the thou-sand for the Union — to beat the alarm and the rally in combat, cheer the miles of marching, or mark a slower tempo for songs of home. From tough-fibered New England villages such as East Topsham, Vermont (left), young men took their town-meeting ideals of democracy with them into war.

35

the powerful industrial North? The answer seemed quite clear on the face of it. None. Omitting the deeply divided border states of Kentucky and Missouri, five and a half million white Southerners faced a total white population of some twenty million. The Union boasted more than eight out of ten factories, more than 70 percent of railroad mileage, all the fighting ships, and most of the money.

What the South did have was faith and a consummate will to fight: faith in its cause and the will that springs like a well of strength when one's homeland must be defended. These were enough; the paraphernalia of war would follow.

For all its economic and industrial might, the North itself was unprepared for war. As of December 1860 the puny United States Army mustered only 16,367 officers and men, almost all of them scattered on the western frontier; no force whatsoever was available to take the field. The United States Navy had some 9,000 officers and men on its rolls, and wooden craft comprised the fleet — only 42 of them in commission, most of them in far waters. On March 4, 1861, only three warships were available on the east coast.

Both sides, then, had to tool up. Agents soon roamed Europe purchasing weapons and other accouterments of battle. Contracts by the hundreds were awarded to Northern manufacturers for everything from ammunition, blankets, buttons, caskets, and medical supplies to musical instruments, swords, tents, uniforms, and watches. Eventually, the South also built up its own industrial capacity and sources of supply — but by no means ever enough.

So the dogs of war were fed; and several times, it seems, the Confederacy came close to victory, within a saber's slash of forcing the Union to let its willful sisters pursue their destiny independently, *if only....*

"If only...." People still utter the words like a litany; for some, the old agonies will never end. I have met men and women North, West, and South who, when they get easy with you, unburden their hearts. They say that what their fathers and grandfathers and uncles and great-uncles fought for a century and more ago, they believe in today. I would reply that this land seldom has been of a single mind about anything. The great point is that today's divisiveness reverberates within a united Nation. That's what the Civil War was all about.

As a man who lives in the wrong century, I enjoyed finding signs of ante bellum America. In New England, the Midwest, and below the Mason-Dixon line I felt at home in towns that wear the trappings of contemporary civilization only casually.

I readily imagined them without paved streets and electricity. I gladly replaced their automobiles and trucks with buggies and wagons. I tore down the television antennas, and leveled the insipid new structures that pose as architecture. And I strolled into the mid-19th century: Main Street and Church Street; village green and town square; gabled and corniced early Victorian houses with fine wide porches; white-pillared courthouses and mansions.

Massachusetts provided a delightful example of the continuity between Civil War times and ours. I came upon it driving west from Springfield into the time-rounded upthrusts of the Berkshire Hills. Nestling in a secluded valley, little changed from the day it was in-

N.G.S. PHOTOGRAPHER JOSEPH J. SCHERSCHEL

In this house at 121 High Street, Galena, Illinois, U.S. Grant and his family lived while he worked in his father's leather shop after 4½ years of failure as a farmer. He struck neighbors as a sad man — taciturn, shabby, and stooped. After Lincoln called citizens to the Union's defense, Grant received a commission and helped organize his state's volunteers.

Golden hand on the spire of the First Presbyterian Church points heavenward for the people of Port Gibson, Mississippi. The rich cotton town escaped damage in 1863 when Grant battled Rebels on its outskirts in his campaign to take Vicksburg.

corporated in 1754, lies the town of Granville, population 874. About 1850, a Granville farmer named Silas Noble took the notion to make a drum. He liked his handiwork, and so did James P. Cooley, a local man of means. They organized the firm of Noble & Cooley and began producing the instrument.

Noble & Cooley still turns out drums, and some of its artisans are descendants of the original workers.

When I called on John B. Jones, the company's energetic vice president, he handed me the diary kept by Mr. Cooley and pointed to a faded entry dated "Sat 18 Aug 1860." I read it at a glance: "Fine day Finished the Lincoln Drum to-day The finest thing ever made."

"That's a good story for you," Mr. Jones said. "Back in 1860, we sent to Illinois and got a rail that Lincoln supposedly had split. From it we carved one of the most expensive military-size drums ever made, with hooks of pure silver and a cord of silk — red, white, and blue. Then we shipped it to Lincoln and it thumped the beat in his campaign for President. Later it was presented to the 10th Massachusetts Regiment."

Business boomed when the Civil War began, the young executive continued. Many a soldier stepped off to the rat-a-tat-tat of Noble & Cooley drums. They couldn't be fashioned rapidly enough by hand, and machinery took over. In 1854 the fledgling firm built 631 drums; in 1863, about 58,000.

"Getting back to the Lincoln drum," I prompted, "who has it now?"

"We wish we knew," replied Mr. Jones. "If you can find it, we'll gladly refurbish it free of charge. There's never been a drum like it."

The fortunes of towns I stopped in vary like the fortunes of men. Granville follows its slow, even course. Galena, Illinois, once a plangent river port and mining center and the home of an obscure clerk named Ulysses S. Grant, lives on its faded memories as "The Town That Time Forgot." The lead deposits eventually played out, river traffic died, and Grant had departed for greater things.

Atlanta, Georgia, a rail hub of 10,000 persons in 1860, captured and gutted four years later, today astounds the eye and ear with its explosive energy. Beaufort, South Carolina, ante bellum haven of wealthy coastal planters, deserted by them as the Federals drew near, quietly keeps company with the cotton kings' fine houses and shows them proudly to visitors during annual tours.

THE GRACIOUS OLD SOUTH lives on too at Natchez, Mississippi, famous for its many elegant mansions. One forgets today's cares wandering through them and resting in their gardens amidst the gentle splendor of azaleas and camellias and the perfume of boxwood.

"How romantic," sighed my wife. I disliked breaking the spell, but the South's magnolia-and-mint-julep mystique can use some debunking. Few ladies wore finery imported from Europe and directed large retinues of servants; only a small number of men were merchant princes or booted gallants on horseback who ruled thousands of acres and followed the chivalric code.

"Let's drive up the Natchez Trace to Port Gibson," I suggested to Jane, "and see the kind of town that served the South's other 90 percent."

Jane, the children, and I covered the 40 miles in as many minutes and slowed when Port Gibson's numerous spires pierced the sky along broad, tree-veiled Church Street. "Look up," I said, and Robbie, Meredith, and Julia blinked in surprise: Atop the First Presbyterian Church's soaring steeple, a gigantic golden hand pointed a stern index finger heavenward.

I have been a Port Gibson admirer for years, having visited there several times on previous NATIONAL GEOGRAPHIC assignments in the area. I find it ever changeless, as much the quiet market town and county seat today as when General Grant came through on his way to Vicksburg and—so local tradition says—called it "too beautiful to burn."

I agree. Port Gibson *is* beautiful. As it has since the late 1700's, it reposes above the banks of Bayou Pierre, eight miles east of the Mississippi. Flatboats at first and then stern-wheelers and small side-wheelers from St. Louis and New Orleans once lined the shore. Small farmers and large planters alike carried the yield of their fields to Port Gibson and sent it off up and down the Father of Waters. Later, railroads helped make the town a hub of commerce.

T ODAY MANY OF PORT GIBSON'S nearly 3,000 residents bear the names of pioneer families, and perhaps half the buildings antedate the Civil War. On Main Street, the Port Gibson Bank, built in 1840 in the classic Greek tradition, continues in use. Nearby, the Planters Hotel, erected in 1817, still stands, now an apartment house. I should like to have sampled its hospitality, judging from the report of a guest in 1828:

"The Steward . . . comes to the parlor door at the dining hour with carving knife and fork crossed before his broad breast, face glowing with smiles, clad in snowy, stiffly starched apron, and says, 'Good evening, ladies fair, Generals and Captains; walk in and partake of barbecued venison, pork, beef, roast turkey, stuffed duck, geese, fish from the biggest river on earth; chicken salad, shrimps and crabs killed in duds for the approval of beautiful ladies' appetites, cakes and jellies for the married, cold potato custard for those in love; gin from Holland; wines from France and Spain. Come one and all. Eat and drink all that you can contain.'"

Perhaps the life was too good to last. One day Grant's army would arrive to fight its way past Port Gibson and then sweep on. King Cotton succumbed. But the good land and its people came back. In the fullness of time, cattle and hogs, soybeans, lumber, and cotton to a lesser degree have become the area's economic backbone. Beneath it all, old Port Gibson's steady pulse keeps time.

But in the 1850's, it was cotton that led the states of the lower South to think they could make a go of it as a separate nation. The world needed cotton, and the South provided three-fourths of the supply. The Industrial Revolution fed the demand. England, proclaimed a Southern Senator, "would topple headlong, and carry the whole civilized world with her" if cotton were not available. To back up this grievously mistaken conviction, the South was willing to fight.

Before the War: Oak Alley, a prosperous Louisiana sugar plantation, flourished like other large estates by the Mississippi, providing for a few an opulent life, and for many the legend of an Old South dream world, both fiery and easygoing.

39

1861:
BATTLES FOR THE BORDER

CHAPTER TWO

ABRAHAM LINCOLN, 52 years old, tall and plain-spoken and fond of telling jokes, took office on March 4, 1861. Born in Kentucky, raised on the fast-changing frontier, self-educated, he had practiced law and served in the Illinois state legislature and for one term as a member of Congress (1847-49). His debates in 1858 with Stephen A. Douglas on sectionalism and slavery made him a national figure and led to the Presidency. He took power boldly and used it with wisdom and humility.

Even as he repeated the Presidential oath, the month-old Confederacy readied a call for 100,000 volunteers. But Lincoln did not consider the seven seceded states as actually having left the Union. In his Inaugural Address, he uttered a heartfelt appeal to all Americans: "Though passion may have strained, it must not break our bonds of affection."

It was too late. Lincoln must have known. Out in Charleston's fine harbor sat Fort Sumter, Federal stronghold guarding the entrances. With each soft Southern dawn the obstinate fort posed a fresh insult to the Confederacy, which meant to obtain it by negotiation — or force. By now, nearly all United States installations in the cotton states had been seized. Here Civil War at last would flame.

I took my family across Charleston Harbor to Fort Sumter one bright morning, sailing in strong sunlight and a spanking breeze with a boatload of tourists. The fort, on a man-made island of rock built on a shoal, spreads over only 2.4 acres; Robbie stood beside the main flagpole on the small parade ground and surveyed the damage wrought by battering shot and shell. He jumped when I told him that it all started precisely over his head. At 4:30 a.m. on April 12, 1861, a mortar flashed on shore and its deadly missile arched through the darkness — lighted fuse flashing as the iron ball revolved — to explode squarely over the fort, where the flagpole now rises.

Within minutes shore batteries ringing the harbor opened fire. They kept it up for 34 hours. Brig. Gen. Pierre G. T. Beauregard, CSA, poured more than 3,000 shells into the fort. Maj. Robert Anderson, USA, fired back as best he could.

The spectacle thrilled Charleston. Business halted. Gaudily caparisoned military men, few of whom had ever known the sight and sound of battle, watched from wharves and ships. Hoop-skirted ladies with dainty parasols thronged the Battery and cheered for the cannonade.

Meredith, our 7-year-old, perked up her ears at this. Perched on a cannon, she asked, "What made the guns stop?"

"Major Anderson surrendered," I said. "It was pointless to fight on. The fact that he and Beauregard knew each other probably made things easier." Anderson had taught years earlier at the United States

Romance brightened the high ideals that sent young men to conflict: for a perpetual Union, as in "The Consecration, 1861," or for independence. As one veteran from the North would recall many years afterward, "...in our youth our hearts were touched with fire...."

GEORGE C. LAMBDIN, 1865,
BERRY-HILL GALLERIES, INC., NEW YORK CITY

Shellbursts from the South Carolina shore batter Fort Sumter before dawn, April 12. This strong-hold, occupied by a small Union garrison, dominated Charleston Harbor; after weeks of demand-

ing its possession, Confederates resorted to force. The contemporary artist exaggerated the guns and
put troops into action about two hours too early, but conveyed the shock of those first irrevocable shots.

NATIONAL GEOGRAPHIC PHOTOGRAPHER EMORY KRISTOF (ABOVE); MARTHA COOPER GUTHRIE

Fort Sumter, today maintained as a national monument, stands on her artificial rock-built island. At right, the author and his family stop in a casemate to let Robbie examine a 42-pounder smoothbore, one of the fort's original cannon. The bombardment of Fort Sumter meant to the North and West a last and intolerable insult from the arrogant "slave power." Lincoln called 75,000 militia into national service. Four states—Virginia, North Carolina, Arkansas, and Tennessee—answered by seceding to join the newly organized Confederacy. Elsewhere, in profound anger and devotion, Northerners vowed to defend the Union.

44

Military Academy; Cadet Beauregard studied artillery under him, and obviously learned his lessons well. Now he offered generous terms: Anderson and his men could evacuate the fort with their arms and personal baggage, they could salute the United States flag, and they could take a steamer to New York.

On April 14 Fort Sumter's proud garrison marched out. The band played "Yankee Doodle," and a 50-gun salute preceded the lowering of Old Glory. One cannon discharged prematurely, killing a gunner and mortally wounding another. Theirs were the only lives lost.

Fort Sumter fell on a Sunday. Next day, Lincoln called out 75,000 militia. They would serve 90 days to suppress powerful combinations opposing the laws of the United States. A little later, the President ordered a blockade of Southern ports.

Virginia, North Carolina, Tennessee, and Arkansas angrily refused to furnish men "for making war on the South." They seceded. When they joined the Confederacy, it became a powerful entity for the first time. It comprised 11 states, increased its population by about 80 percent, gained ironworks and other vital industry, and acquired a buffer to protect the lower states while they developed an industrial base.

The cold war had ended. Sword and bullet would settle the matter.

With the outbreak of hostilities came a sense of relief in the South, a furious indignation in the North. Martial ardor swept the land. Lincoln called for volunteers to serve three years. By the tens of thousands young men signed up. North and South, recruiters opened offices in vacant stores and pitched tents in town squares.

In New Orleans, the Confederacy's largest city, men in civilian clothes counted cadence to shrill fife and rattling drum, drilling while tailors labored around the clock turning out colorful uniforms. Ladies young and not-so-young pitched in, sewing cartridge bags from red flannel, rolling bandages, making shirts and underclothing.

In New York City, gay throngs had already bidden farewell to the 7th New York as that regiment set off to protect the Nation's Capital. Girls fluttered kerchiefs and tossed kisses and the kid-gloved 7th loved it, cocky in its smart, crossbelted gray tunics.

Those were the good days, and they were few. Plenty of people thought the struggle would not last long. Who could foresee ragged, barefoot soldiers stripping clothes and shoes from the bodies of fallen foes? Who could predict the specter of near-starvation, the typhoid that scythed fresh-faced country boys?

America's most promising soldier, Robert E. Lee, envisioned the long, grim road ahead. So did his superior and great admirer, Lt. Gen. Winfield Scott, who stood — or perhaps I should say sat, for he was aged and infirm and quite fat — at the head of the United States Army. General Scott, hero of the War of 1812 and the War with Mexico, was almost 75, "a year older than the Constitution" as wags remarked. He would resign on November 1, 1861. Before retiring, however, he would devise the "Anaconda Plan" which, though never officially adopted, contained the seeds of the winning strategy.

Scott's design relied on the naval blockade to keep Southern ports closed, strangling the Confederacy. Meanwhile, Union gunboats and troopships would curl down the Mississippi Valley "so as to envelop

In serried ranks a Union regiment turns smartly during a drill in 1861. The colorful dress shows French influence; without a fully standardized uniform until 1863, the Army permitted volunteer

JAMES WALKER, 1861, WEST POINT MUSEUM, ALEXANDER McCOOK CRAIGHEAD COLLECTION

units to choose their own. Throughout the war infantry often attacked in drill formation — long suc-cessive lines of men moving in view of the enemy, a tactic outmoded by improved rifles and cannon.

the insurgent States and bring them to terms with less bloodshed than by any other plan"—a reasonable but foredoomed hope.

Robbie wondered why it took the North so long to make the plan work. I spread out a map of the United States and drew a border around the Confederacy. "Inside the border," I told him, "lies a region of mountains and plains, deserts, swamps, valleys—all kinds of terrain with few towns and fewer cities. It covers 750,000 square miles. That's the territory the Union had to subdue."

I ran a finger along the jagged coastline from Virginia's northern border around Florida's southern tip to Texas. "The United States Navy had to maintain a 4,000-mile patrol."

The water war's extent and importance is not appreciated by most of us, I believe. As the Union blockade tightened, it gradually choked the South's war machine, marking the first effective use in modern times of warships to produce economic ruin. Confederate blockade-runners—lean, swift, ghostly vessels—were pursued in distant waters, and United States men-of-war battled Southern cruisers over most of the oceans.

Besides the war at sea, military historians point to three arenas of land war: the eastern, western, and trans-Mississippi theaters. Here again, a map helps dispel geographic confusion about the Civil War. In the eastern theater—the land from the Appalachian Mountains to the Atlantic—occurred much of the fighting. On the other hand, the western theater—between the Appalachians and the Mississippi River—decided the war's outcome, which hinged on control of the river. Beyond it, the trans-Mississippi provided food for the Confederacy.

Old General Scott traced this pattern when he drew up his Anaconda Plan. It might have produced the South's downfall sooner had Robert E. Lee accepted an invitation to take command of the new Union army.

As WAR BREAKS OUT, we see a Lee most of us do not recognize. He is 54 years old, with 36 years of distinguished service to his country behind him. A tall, dark-haired, handsome and imposing Virginian, second in his class at West Point, he moves with composure and quiet authority. Four years of war take their toll before he becomes the man most of us know—the old, worn, white-bearded father-figure of Mathew Brady's magnificent photograph, with strength still in his eyes, and sorrow too. But in all the war years Lee will not make a more difficult decision than he must make now. He loves his country, this patrician and son of patricians, and dislikes the idea of disunion. He simply believes first of all in Virginia. Duty binds him to his state. In a letter to his Unionist sister, Anne Lee Marshall of Baltimore, he speaks his mind:

"With all my devotion to the Union and the feeling of loyalty and duty of an American citizen I have not been able to make up my mind to raise my hand against my relatives, my children, my home. I have therefore resigned my commission in the Army, and save in defense of my native State (with the sincere hope that my poor services may never be needed) I hope I may never be called upon to draw my sword."

This excruciating dilemma drove many men to follow their state and not their flag. It separated families and brought the tragedy of father fighting son, of brother fighting brother—civil war is the cruelest war. "I know you will blame me," wrote Lee to his sister, "but you must think

Advertisements showing flashy Zouave uniforms, modeled after those of a French-Algerian drill team that toured the country in 1860, attracted flocks of eager volunteers. At first, contingents of both sides wore Zouave costumes—pantaloons, sashes, turbans, and leggings—but such finery soon gave way to more practical apparel. The 114th Pennsylvania Regiment, recruited partly by the poster at left, managed to retain its bright dress throughout the war.

of me as kindly as you can and believe that I have endeavored to do what I thought right."

His native state promptly called him to her service. The Potomac was Lee's Rubicon; he crossed over to accept command, as major general, of Old Dominion land and naval forces. For a year he would labor in a kind of oblivion, trying to coordinate forces in Virginia's far reaches, helping fortify the east coast, and advising the imperious Jefferson Davis.

Kentucky-born, Davis grew up in Mississippi and graduated from West Point in 1828, a year ahead of Lee. Later a Mississippi planter, he was elected to Congress in 1845. He resigned to fight in the Mexican War, in which he was severely wounded and won a hero's praise. Later he became a Senator, and Secretary of War under Franklin Pierce.

Davis, age 52, now stood at the Confederacy's head, trying to run a revolution by constitutional means, trying to build a victorious central government for 11 sovereign states. So sensitive that even a child's disapproval could upset him, so high-minded that compromise came hard to him, he gave himself completely to his country, hiding a flaming courage behind a stiff and chilly dignity. Legalistic to the end, he meant to be literally Commander-in-Chief as well as President; he quarreled with generals he disliked, and remained as loyal to some mediocre officers as he was to the selfless and diplomatic Lee.

April slipped into May and the day after Virginians ratified secession Union soldiers crossed the Potomac to occupy Alexandria and Arlington Heights, chasing Rebel pickets away. Queen Victoria proclaimed Great Britain's neutrality while recognizing the Confederacy as a belligerent. Napoleon III soon announced the same for France.

Fighting began as June arrived; before it was over, Blue and Gray would test one another in more than 2,000 battles, engagements, and skirmishes. The first of any size took place at Philippi in western Virginia, on June 3. Federals under 34-year-old Maj. Gen. George B. McClellan, soon famous as "the young Napoleon," routed some 1,500 Southerners with small losses on either side. A week later at Big Bethel Church on Virginia's Peninsula—between the James River and the York—Confederates returned the favor, driving a disordered party of attacking Yankees back in confusion.

49

The preliminaries had ended. Richmond, the Confederacy's newly-chosen Capital, beckoned invitingly only a hundred miles south of Washington. Already Mr. Lincoln coveted the Rebel city with a yearning that would know frustration almost to the war's last gun.

The lone railroad approach to Richmond from the North was blocked at Manassas Junction, Virginia, a small cluster of houses about 25 miles southwest of the District of Columbia. General Beauregard, Fort Sumter's dashing, egocentric victor, had been ordered by President Davis to defend Manassas, and he was getting ready.

"On to Richmond," exhorted the press. "Action!" cried North and South alike, though their soldiers were unready. On July 16 the Union commander, Brig. Gen. Irvin McDowell, reluctantly set a few Regulars and around 35,000 raw recruits in motion out of their camps near Washington. Most of these were the President's 90-day militia, and their tours were almost up; war was a lark. They ambled toward Manassas as to a picnic; the first day's advance covered only six miles.

It must have been an astonishing sight—an unkempt line of march expanding and contracting over dusty roads like a caterpillar, with national and regimental flags fluttering at the head of each colorful gaggle of troops: Fire Zouaves sporting red fezzes, short blue jackets, and baggy red pantaloons; the Garibaldi Guard jaunty in its green-plumed hats; even a lively bunch of Highlanders, though they wore blue pants for this occasion instead of their parade kilts.

General McDowell never forgot that procession. "They stopped every moment," he recalled incredulously, "to pick blackberries, or get water; they would not keep in the ranks, order as you pleased. . . ."

I described the march to my family as we drove one Sunday afternoon to Manassas National Battlefield Park, a pleasant half-hour journey from our Maryland home. McDowell's mention of blackberries reminded 5-year-old Julia, an excellent trencherman, that she was hungry.

"You should have seen what the spectators were eating," I told her.

Spectators? Just so. Several hundred citizens, including Senators, Representatives, and some ladies of blithe spirit, stripped Washington of picnic lunches and sallied forth as the big battle drew near. They rattled along in holiday mood, their carriages, gigs, wagons, and hacks tossing up clouds of dust. McDowell was going to thrash his West Point classmate Beauregard and the Rebels once and for all. This had to be the spectacle of a lifetime. And it was. It was.

Two and a half days after the army left camp, having strolled a little more than 20 miles, it came up to the hamlet of Centreville. Three miles southwest trickled the waters of Bull Run; several miles beyond the stream sat Manassas Junction, springboard to Richmond.

The difficulty was that General Beauregard waited on Bull Run's south bank, defending about seven winding miles. He now mustered 32,000 Southerners; 9,000 of them had just arrived from the Shenandoah Valley—under forced march and then by rail—with Gen. Joseph E. Johnston at their head. Some of these men didn't quite know what to think of their brigade commander, a dour, lean, religious, lemon-sucking disciplinarian named Thomas J. Jackson, recently a mediocre teacher at the Virginia Military Institute. They soon would learn.

Hastening to a tense Washington, D.C., the 7th New York Militia entrains at Jersey City on April 19. Rebels in Maryland and Virginia threatened the Capital, and when the regiment arrived, Lincoln "smiled all over," a soldier wrote. One of the few fully equipped and trained units at war's outbreak, the force of nearly a thousand men helped guard the city during 45 critical days.

You can still stand, as we did, in the lines along Bull Run. You can walk to the wooded crest of Signal Hill and look for miles across the same gently swelling plateau that the Southerners saw. Imagine now. Peel back the century and picture Confederate soldiers at Signal Hill. Glance northwest eight miles to Sudley Ford—*what glints there when you put glass to eye?* The sharp morning sun throws darts against a brass fieldpiece, glittering bayonets, and burnished rifle barrels; Federals are turning the South's left flank, sneaking around behind it. Frantically the signals officer waves his newfangled flags: "Look out for your left; you are turned." Warfare's first wigwag message proves successful.

Francis F. Wilshin, then superintendent of Manassas National Battle-field Park, conducted us over the ground. No one knows what happened here better than he; for 14 years Mr. Wilshin *Continued on page 56*

Continued on page 56

Off-duty crewmen of U.S.S. Mendota, *on station in the James River, take a moment from checkers and banjo-playing for something rare and special: their photograph. This ship, a side-wheeler designed especially for river service, began her career late in the war, when the Union controlled most*

Southern coasts and inland waters. The Navy had only three men-of-war on the East Coast in 1861 when Lincoln proclaimed a blockade; it rapidly acquired, constructed, and re-commissioned ships to shut Confederate ports and keep out desperately needed war supplies sent from Europe.

WILLIAM TORGERSON, WEST POINT MUSEUM, ALEXANDER McCOOK CRAIGHEAD COLLECTION (ABOVE), AND BURK UZZLE

Confederate blockade-runners—fast, low-lying, painted off-white for minimal visibility at sea— anchor at St. George's, Bermuda; lighters took their cotton ashore in trade for medicines, war matériel, and prized luxuries brought by dark- hulled freighters from Britain. By mid-1863 two- thirds of the Southern stock of arms had come from abroad. The 150-pound lead pigs at left, the raw

material of bullets, went down with a British
steamer off Fort Fisher, North Carolina, in 1862.
A century later, Navy divers recovered the oxi-
dized metal, along with bullet molds and Enfield
rifles. High profits lured some captains to blockade-
running; duty called others, such as John N. Maf-
fitt, CSN, to risk their lives running arms as
well as inflicting heavy losses on Union shipping.

Col. Robert E. Lee, USA: As a young officer in the small Regular Army of the 1840's, Lee won high recognition and three citations for gallantry for his exploits in the Mexican War. He served from 1852 to 1855 as Superintendent of West Point. On April 18, 1861, he received an offer from Lincoln: Would he command the great new army of the Union? No. He could take no part in action against his state. After deep inner conflict he sadly resigned his commission, loyal to Virginia and — as by his family motto (on crest, opposite) — "not unmindful of the future."

virtually lived on the field. "From 9:30 a.m. to 3 p.m.," he told us, "the battle was touch-and-go, depending on how fast reinforcements reached either side." A dramatic instance of this occurred in late morning as fresh Federal troops came up and hammered at a shaky Confederate position. Then, says tradition, with his men about to run, Brig. Gen. Barnard Bee waved at the hill where Jackson's brigade braced strong and resolute against the Union sweep. "There stands Jackson like a stone wall!" Bee shouted. "Rally on the Virginians!"

After Bull Run, Stonewall Jackson's men knew what to think of him.

Near Centreville, the holidaying throng crowded fields and clogged the road, cheering as riders dashed back from the front with good tidings. William Howard Russell, correspondent of *The Times* of London, offered his flask to a soldier. That worthy took "a startling pull, which left little between the bottom and utter vacuity," Russell noted sourly.

"The fact is," Superintendent Wilshin told us as we paused where the confident sightseers had, "most of the fighting was taking place six miles from here. They could hear the rumble of cannon and the faint firecracker roll of musket fire, but they couldn't see the flashes."

The picnickers found out soon enough what really was going on. Union victory indeed had seemed near as afternoon wore on. Then a fresh Rebel brigade of Johnston's hit the Federal right flank. As it crumbled, Beauregard renewed a general attack along the line.

Suddenly the battle played itself out. The Yankees began falling back. Under artillery fire the dispiriting sense of debacle took hold, and with it terrifying anticipation of onrushing Rebel cavalry, sabers on high. Retreat turned into rout. McDowell had ordered his army to regroup at Centreville, but panic-stricken troops crashed through the little town and the civilian sojourners plunged into the crush. In headlong flight they made for Washington; rain pelted down on a hurly-burly of careening carriages and army supply wagons and staggering, exhausted men.

Lincoln stayed up all night at the White House listening to first-hand accounts. Now Beauregard might invade Washington! But the Southerners, disorganized themselves, did not press their advantage. Throughout the war, each side often would fail to give the *coup de grâce*.

I asked Mr. Wilshin to assess this first major battle. "It told the North," he replied, "that a real war lay ahead. It humiliated the Union, and strengthened its resolve. The North went to work. As for the South, victory at Bull Run produced great elation, and with it a false sense of security and overconfidence."

And what of those who died at Bull Run, I asked. We walked into a silent woodland just south of the park's Visitor Center. Leaves rustled underfoot; the setting sun limned the trees and loaned strange substance to their shadows; a rabbit scampered through the forest litter. "There," spoke my companion. A small mound stood above the woodland floor, brown earth smoothly rounded and laced with leaves. "And there. And there." Several of them. Many.

After the Battle of Bull Run, people from Manassas and Warrenton and all around came looking for the bodies of their sons, searching far into the night by lantern light. No one claimed these men. Few people today know they rest there. No one remembers their names.

"Let them lie in peace where their comrades buried them," said Mr. Wilshin. "This is a special kind of hallowed ground."

Not only at Bull Run, but at any other battlefield, men died unidentified or disappeared without record, and throughout the war reliable figures for casualties were almost never available. Accurate figures for the forces engaged are, if anything, more elusive. Muster rolls may be available, but not all the men listed would be present to fight. Federal reports counted men present for duty; Confederates stressed actual fighting strength. On both sides harried officers made up their figures hurriedly, estimating the number of stragglers on the march. Scholars ever since have studied the problem at length, and their figures often vary by several thousand or so. The confusion of war was not confined to the celebrated battle of July 21, 1861.

McDowell lost his command, though the Union fiasco at Bull Run was not his fault especially, and General McClellan took command of the troops near Washington. Congress authorized an army of 500,000 three-year men and a larger navy. A master at organization and training, McClellan toiled ceaselessly whipping recruits into shape.

"Little Mac" could place some fairly promising men at the head of these troops; no fewer than 63 Union officers who saw action at Bull Run were or would become generals—although not all proved great or even good. Two who would write their names large were an outspoken, red-bearded infantry colonel named William Tecumseh Sherman, age 41, and a yellow-haired cavalryman named George Armstrong Custer, taut as coiled steel, ambitious beyond his mere 21 years.

The Confederacy too discovered many leaders at Bull Run; 54 had or would wear a general's stars. Among them: the fearless, flamboyant James E. B. Stuart, 28, a real *beau sabreur* of mounted infantry, "the eyes of the army"; and tireless James Longstreet, 40, "Old Pete" to his men, Lee's blunt and capable "war horse."

McClellan drilled his farmers and mechanics, dashing about on his noble black charger. Virginia lapsed into uneasy calm. Out in troubled Missouri, most grievously divided border state of all, only a spark was wanting to set off the battle that would decide that state's course. Already Union men under Capt. Nathaniel Lyon had captured a Rebel camp on the outskirts of St. Louis and brought the secession-minded city under Federal control after a riot.

The Confederacy badly needed Missouri. August arrived, and a motley Rebel force of Texans, Louisianians, Arkansans, and Missourians advanced on Springfield: cowboys, cane-brake Cajuns, coonskin-hatted mountain men bearing squirrel guns—about 11,000 of them. At their head rode Maj. Gen. Sterling Price, of Missouri's state guards, who had deferred command to Brig. Gen. Ben McCulloch of Texas, a startling figure in snowy five-gallon hat, boots, and gray velvet coat with yellow cuffs and lapels.

At Springfield, around 5,400 Union men under Nathaniel Lyon, now a brigadier for his good work at St. Louis, marched by night to surprise the Rebels. Johnny Reb and Billy Yank met at dawn in fearful embrace at Wilson's Creek, 10 miles southwest of the city. Five hours of slaughter ensued, and the two sides suffered a combined loss of more than 2,500 casualties, among them General Lyon, wounded twice and then shot dead. The Federals retreated.

McCulloch, lacking supplies, withdrew to Arkansas. Price remained active with his Missourians; the state, however, stayed within the Union —though strife continued to sear it from end to end.

T ODAY THE NEW Wilson's Creek Battlefield National Park sprawls across the rolling land. I flew to Springfield to watch National Park Service personnel re-create the setting of August 10, 1861, and with Park Service management assistant Charles T. Meier forded the swift little stream that gives the site its name. "Back in the 1830's," he said, "James Wilson, a squaw man, trapped along this creek. Farmers began settling on the land a few years later. A short distance from here archeologists found their long-forgotten mill, its old timbers and millstone still in the creek bed."

Mr. Meier swept an arm at a sloping field. "The farmers grew corn and oats and peaches. That's why the Confederates camped here—the corn was ripe, food for horses and men. One group was 'roasting' ears for breakfast in a huge kettle when the Yankees announced themselves.

Fog blurs valleys around Cheat Mountain where minor battles during the summer of 1861 shaped the course of war. Here, beyond the Shenandoah River, the men of Virginia's western counties had long been at odds with tidewater planters and showed no zeal for secession. On May 26, with the Old Dominion out of the Union, Federal forces began crossing the Ohio River to take the mountain area—by order of Maj. Gen. George B. McClellan, a handsome West Point graduate. His men scored a series of successes that inspirited Northern morale, and led Lincoln to call "the young Napoleon" to Washington to build the Army of the Potomac the day after the fiasco at Bull Run. Soon afterward General Lee, CSA, arrived in western Virginia, responsible for coordinating but not for directing four small armies. Feuding among themselves, his subordinates bungled; the South lost part of Virginia, and for a time Lee's fame became shadowed.

59

Rebels in Zouave uniforms charge embattled Union soldiers in this fanciful rendering of the Federals' retreat on July 21 from the fight at Bull Run, only 28 miles from Washington. The Confederates, as

unseasoned as their opponents, made no pursuit. Some Yankees panicked; others withdrew in tolerable order. The defeat, witnessed by a crowd of civilians, belied Northern predictions of a short, easy war.

61

A cannonball hit the kettle dead center and the corn flew high in the air."

The State of Missouri purchased the park's 1,730 acres, enough land to take in the battle's entire sweep. Research pinpointed the location of vanished houses as well as the mill. Post-Civil War farmhouses, barns, silos, and other structures have been removed. The old Ray house, a hospital during the fighting, is undergoing complete restoration.

Tom Meier anticipates that when facilities are complete, tourists by the thousands will turn off nearby Interstate 44 to see the park. A visitor center will welcome them, and color movies will tell Wilson Creek's little-known tale. Park Service representatives will demonstrate camp life—even to firing rifle-muskets—and displays at each battlefield stopping point will enhance the drama. "We hope to make history come alive," said my host in summary.

Odd, I thought as I departed, how history continually crosses paths. Before the war, the Ray house served as a flag stop for the Butterfield Overland Mail, whose stages began rolling in 1858 from Tipton, Missouri, and jolted across 2,700 bone-bending miles via El Paso, Tucson, and Los Angeles to San Francisco.

I myself returned comfortably by air to St. Louis, and found history weaving a fascinating maze at the Old Courthouse, now a museum and headquarters for the Jefferson National Expansion Memorial. I halted on its steps, remembering that slaves had been sold on them. I walked inside; Dred Scott heard his suit for freedom argued in one of these courtrooms. A former Army captain named Grant, scrabbling for a living as a businessman, freed his only slave here.

Samuel Clemens, better known as Mark Twain, sighted on the Courthouse's cast-iron dome as he piloted steamboats toward the wide levee. When the war began, he cast his lot briefly with the South, and

WILLIAM EPPRIDGE

Tired Union volunteer, right in character for a centennial re-enactment of the First Battle of Bull Run, cools his feet on a scorching July day. Rebel infantry (left) prepare to attack an enemy battery; horse artillerymen in action sponge the barrel of a 12-pounder Napoleon, ram the charge of another, and prepare to fire.

then departed for more congenial employment as a newspaperman in the West. One day, as a prominent publisher, Clemens would give the world Grant's excellent *Personal Memoirs*, a two-volume best-seller.

Ulysses S. Grant, was a most uncommon man. An Ohio farm boy, he graduated from West Point 21st in his class of 39, a quiet and unassuming fellow. "Nobody would have picked him out as one who was destined to occupy a conspicuous place in history," recalled a classmate.

Grant fought well in the Mexican War, winning two citations for bravery. Serving in California in 1854, he penned a homesick letter to his wife: "I sometimes get so anxious to see you, and our little boys, that I am almost tempted to resign...." Finding the separation unendurable, he quit the Army and took up farming near St. Louis. In 1858, stricken with ague, he left the land and tried unsuccessfully to support his wife and four children in real estate. In 1860, the Grant family rode a steamer up-Mississippi to Galena, Illinois. There he clerked in his father's leather store for $800 a year, a defeated man to all appearances.

When Lincoln called for troops, civilian Grant drilled Galena's company of enlistees but declined to captain them, believing himself qualified to command a regiment. He offered his services to the War Department, and his letter was mislaid. Over in Cincinnati, General McClellan, whom he had known at West Point and in the Mexican War, was marshaling Ohio troops; Grant, seeking a position on McClellan's staff, called twice at his office on successive days but never got to see him.

Governor Richard Yates of Illinois appointed Grant colonel in June 1861, and gave him an infantry regiment. Soon he was promoted to brigadier general of volunteers. Grant's march to military greatness gained impetus with his first star, though the promotion surprised him, as he said, "very much"—he learned of it in a St. Louis newspaper.

Thirty-nine years old, medium of height, spare of frame, a pipe-smoker given to few words, the new general received command of Federal forces in southeastern Missouri and southern Illinois with headquarters at Cairo, Illinois, where the Mississippi and Ohio Rivers join. The Union was concentrating troops there.

On September 4, Confederate Maj. Gen. Leonidas Polk—a West Point friend of Jefferson Davis and peacetime Episcopal Bishop of Louisiana, who strapped on his sword again when war came—seized the town of Columbus, Kentucky. That border state's proclaimed "neutrality" soon proved impossible; Kentucky remained within the Union.

General Grant countered almost immediately. He loaded 1,800

Firing on advancing Rebels at Wilson's Creek, near Springfield, Missouri, loyal troops fight vigorously to save the state from the Confederacy. On August 10, after a morning of hard action in which the Union's Brig. Gen. Nathaniel Lyon died, the outnumbered Yankees retreated. Rebels remained active in parts of Missouri—but the state remained in the Union.

troops aboard transports at Cairo, protected them with three wooden gunboats converted from steamers, and paddle-wheeled about 45 miles up the Ohio to occupy Paducah. His bold move gave the North control of the mouths of the Tennessee and Cumberland Rivers, highways leading into the South's heart. Grant meant to travel those highways.

First, however, he would taste defeat in a clash with Polk at Belmont, Missouri, and gunboats would rescue him and his men from that trap. Then he would have to whip the Confederate commander in the west, Lt. Gen. Albert Sidney Johnston, whose line of defense outran his resources. It extended 600 miles from Columbus on the Mississippi to Fort Henry on the Tennessee and Fort Donelson on the Cumberland,

Union troops brought up by side-wheelers in September land on Kentucky soil—vainly proclaimed neutral by the state

Brigadier General Grant, an obscure figure commanding southeast Missouri, made his headquarters at Cairo, Illinois (right), then a fever-ridden town of some 2,000 people and good rail connections. Using transports and gunboats, he began operations to control the blue Ohio and the muddy Mississippi—quickly employing his flotilla to secure a grip on Kentucky.

to Bowling Green, Kentucky, on to Cumberland Gap in the Alleghenies.

Ships were vital. Already a western flotilla was taking shape at St. Louis and Mound City. Four thousand men worked furiously on round-the-clock shifts building shallow-draught ironclad gunboats.

While the river fleet grew apace, the ocean service also progressed. Union ships slowly began tightening the blockade. Down on the North Carolina coast, a Federal amphibious assault captured Hatteras Inlet, a haven both for blockade-runners and Rebel privateers. Late in October the mightiest armada assembled in America to that time, 75 ships and 169 guns, put out from Hampton Roads, Virginia, to seize and secure a new base for the fleet. Aboard were 12,653 soldiers; surfboats; huge stores of ammunition; building equipment and supplies, even to blacksmith's coal; and about 1,500 horses, with oats to feed them.

Flag Officer Samuel F. du Pont and Brig. Gen. Thomas W. Sherman (called "the other Sherman" before the end of the war) headed the joint force bound for Port Royal Sound, about midway between Charleston and Savannah, Georgia.

I am grateful for their selection; the unsung battle at Hilton Head fascinates me, and the lusty city that sprang up in its wake, only to die, still casts a spell. With my family, I have looked out from Hilton Head Island's northeast tip and conjured up ghostly men-of-war circling in Port Royal Sound's entrance channel. Passing one way, their salvos smash into Rebel troops at Fort Walker, where I stand, and the compliment is returned; swinging around, their broadsides make it hot for Fort Beauregard's defenders, across the channel on Bay Point.

It is only a matter of time, but time is Hilton Head's great story. Within a few hours the Confederates must abandon their battered works. Yankees wade ashore and meet no enemy. Soon a greatly enlarged base begins rising, headquarters for the Army's Department of the South.

In Washington, a pleased Lincoln suggests that Congress tender a vote of thanks to Du Pont. Much of the war has gone badly so far for the Union. The victory at Hilton Head will ease the pain of the defeat at Bull Run and a more recent disaster at Ball's Bluff, on the Potomac.

For the conflict's duration, troop transports shifting men between the fighting fronts will put in to Port Royal Sound to re-provision, and blockaders will sail out to get an ever-firmer chokehold on Rebel ports. Already nearby Savannah and Charleston feel the pinch.

Today, carrying all this in one's head, one visits Hilton Head's northern shore with a sense of wonder. Only Nature commands this quietude. The sprawling plantations of ante bellum days have vanished almost without a sign. A fragment of Fort Walker still stands, its crumbling bricks losing a last battle to wind and water and lush vegetation.

In its heyday, many thousands of uniformed men and civilians, innumerable Negroes from the deserted plantations among them, lived in the fort and its newborn suburbs. The first black soldiers drilled at Hilton Head. Transient soldiers and sailors dined at the Port Royal House, attended the theater, perused two newspapers, got their picture taken, slaked their thirst, and some visited the tattooer. On Christmas Day, 1862, the 47th New York played the 48th New York for the baseball championship at Hilton Head, with an estimated 40,000 fans looking on. I do not know who won.

gislature — to finish a strategic fort.

Of all this virtually nothing remains. Instead, one of the country's finest seaside resort communities graces Hilton Head. People relax on the sandy headland's white beaches and play golf on its excellent courses and the past, overlooked, seems meaningless. Perhaps it is just as well. Jane and the girls love to wander among wildflowers blooming above the shore, and I think them nicely complemented by the primroses and violets and daisies.

But Robbie and I pause at the marker near the fort. It honors two South Carolinians, Thomas Fenwick Drayton, Brigadier General, CSA, and his brother Comdr. Percival Drayton, USN. They met at the outbreak of hostilities, shook hands, and each went the way of his conscience. Thomas chose his state, Percival his flag. Robbie reads the last of the inscription aloud: "On Nov. 7, 1861, the brothers met in battle. Commander Percival Drayton on the gunboat Pocahontas attacked Fort Walker of which General Thomas Drayton was in command."

S TRANGE WAR. For the North, the first year of struggle, with all its discouraging failures, ended in an oddity that nearly brought it to grief in a frenzy of popular excitement.

The Confederacy had named two former United States Senators as Special Commissioners to the powers whose help she needed most. James M. Mason of Virginia—whose authorship of the 1850 Fugitive Slave Law would not strengthen his influence, whose tobacco-chewing habits would repel society—was to serve in England, the more polished John Slidell of Louisiana in France. En route, aboard the British mail steamer *Trent* out of Nassau, they were removed by Capt. Charles Wilkes, USN, commanding U.S.S. *San Jacinto,* and taken to Boston for a cell in Fort Warren. A jubilant press and public hailed Wilkes as a hero; the House of Representatives voted him a gold medal.

Britain felt with justice that her rights had been violated, her honor insulted, her flag degraded. Her Prime Minister cried to his Cabinet: "You may stand for this but damned if I will!" Orders went out to alert a squadron of steam warships, to send 8,000 troops to Canada.

Now Lincoln and his Cabinet faced the most dangerous diplomatic crisis that would ever be their responsibility. Lincoln had never paid much attention to foreign policy, although he had squelched Secretary Seward's plans to reunite the Nation by war with some foreign power. Some of the Cabinet inclined to defend Wilkes and keep the "traitors"; Lincoln soon suspected that they would be a pair of "white elephants."

Perhaps the Confederacy's prospects were never brighter than in the days that Her Majesty's Foreign Office was drafting a harsh protest to the United States, demanding the envoys' release. Yet, on both sides of the Atlantic, statesmen were taking thought. The Prince Consort, so weak from his final illness that he could hardly hold a pen, toned down the draft for Victoria's approval, so that the United States could more readily disclaim responsibility for Wilkes's rash actions. When the British Minister conveyed this message in courteous terms, Lincoln called a special Cabinet meeting. It met at ten o'clock on Christmas morning. All present decided for peace—the British demand was just, and the prisoners would be "cheerfully liberated." Mason and Slidell were soon on their way abroad. Lincoln's policy had prevailed: one war at a time.

U. S. Navy and Army join forces fo

A. R. WAUD, FRANKLIN D. ROOSEVELT LIBRARY (TOP); COMDR. VICTOR M. DAVIS, JR.

he first big amphibious operation of the war: A fleet covers troops wading ashore on Hatteras Island, August 28.

By a victory that the South could never match, Union forces took control of the best entrance to North Carolina's sounds, the route for blockade-runners bringing supplies to the Rebel army in Virginia. Throughout the war the Confederacy found sea power on the Northern scale hopelessly beyond her reach. Today diving teams recover Civil War small arms and ordnance from the waters off the Carolina coast.

The Trent *Affair gives to the Confederacy a few weeks of high hope and to Lincoln, new to international matters, his gravest risk of a misstep. Able but arrogant, Capt. Charles Wilkes, USN (above), runs out the guns of his tall warship* San Jacinto *to halt the British steamer* Trent *and sends a boarding party to remove Confederate diplomats John Slidell and James M. Mason (left and right, below) from the protection of the British flag. He took them to a Boston military prison. His action made him a popular hero at home—and violated the accepted law of nations. Insulted and indignant, Britishers called for the release of the prisoners, with apologies; late in 1861 war fever rose on both sides of the Atlantic.*

Guard forces, part of some 8,000 British troops hastily sent to Canada, march to the border; local guides discuss the best route to follow. Fortunately, the statesmen of Britain and the United States found a way out of the crisis. Britain stated her case firmly, yet courteously. Lincoln and his Cabinet wisely accepted it, complied—and a chance for events that would favor the South had vanished.

1862:
YEAR OF LOST VICTORIES

CHAPTER THREE

WINTER TOOK COMMAND and shut down the war in Virginia, rain and snow converting the roads into impassable sloughs. Bull Run's victors, 47,000 strong, kept dismal house in the mud near Centreville. Their shelters weren't much—huts made of logs, mud, and wood slabs.

The North's growing army polished its bayonets in a hundred smoky bivouacs around Washington. A mighty force assembled one day at Bailey's Cross Roads, only 20 crow-flight miles from the Rebs at Centreville, and thousands of Federals popped to attention when President Lincoln and members of his Cabinet rode down the line in grand review.

Most of the fancy militia uniforms had disappeared. Northern soldiers wore the familiar blue, and Southern troops donned the gray. Both slogged through drills, walked picket, and whiled away spare hours writing letters home ("Dear father and Mother brother and sister it is with pleaseur that I take my pen in hand..."), reading, playing cards, singing, and, always the soldier's solace, sleeping.

McClellan bore the title of General-in-Chief, and his men cheered when he flashed past on his black charger. Others, Lincoln among them, began to wonder if he would ever launch an attack. Press dispatches reported, "All quiet along the Potomac." Murmurs of discontent were heard, and Lincoln did not intend that they should continue. Mindful of a mounting pressure for action, and ever a canny politician, he issued secret orders: All the forces of the Republic would move against the insurgents on February 22, 1862, in honor of Washington's birthday.

Out in Illinois, Ulysses S. Grant was ready to carry out a raid ordered by his superior, Maj. Gen. Henry W. Halleck, and Grant didn't wait for Washington's birthday. Early in February he and Flag Officer Andrew H. Foote, USN, crammed 15,000 soldiers aboard nine river steamer transports, backed them up with four bristling ironclads and three wooden gunboats, and weighed anchor for the Confederacy. Tennessee would reel under war's fury through the war. Here came the beginning.

Target number one was Fort Henry, small and weak, situated in a marsh beside the Tennessee River, 60 miles below Union-held Paducah. A dozen miles to the east, much stronger Fort Donelson guarded the Cumberland River. Invaders trying to ride that water route could count on considerable remonstrance. These two forts keyed the South's entire 600-mile-long line of defense stretching from the Mississippi to the Alleghenies. Turn that key, said Grant, and the Confederacy's door opens.

Foote's transports disgorged the Federals a few miles below Fort Henry. Before they could march up, the ironclads pounded the gallant, half-flooded little earthwork into submission. Most of its 2,610-man garrison escaped to Fort Donelson during the bombardment.

Alert to danger, Union pickets guard a road on the perimeter of their camp. In 1862, fledgling soldiers would learn their trade the hard way—at Donelson and Shiloh, battling for control of western rivers; in Virginia's meadows, contending for the Confederate Capital. By year's end, both sides acknowledged the terrible reality of a long and murderous struggle ahead.

Federal garrison camps on Southern soil beside the Cumberland River, used by gunboats to support a February attac

Curt note (left) conveyed Grant's famous demand for "unconditional surrender" to his prewar army friend Brig. Gen. Simon B. Buckner, Confederate commander of Fort Donelson. Winning the fort, Grant pierced the Confederacy's ambitious western defense line, opening the way to the heart of the South and the occupation of Nashville. Overnight the North hailed Grant a hero. A mounted Federal officer (right) questions a prisoner at Donelson.

n nearby Fort Donelson, Tennessee — early and highly strategic target in Grant's western campaign to split the South.

CENTURY MAGAZINE, 1884

Grant set out from Henry on an unseasonably mild day, and his sweating soldiers shucked blankets and overcoats as they trudged across to Donelson. It was February 12, Lincoln's birthday. Next morning they invested the fort's outer defenses in an arc of nearly three miles, and got down to work. Rain began falling about dusk that evening, drenching the lightly clad Federals. Escorted by a gale, the rain turned to sleet, and then a storm howled down in white fury. Snow thickened on the ground, and some of the companies marched in circles all night to keep warm. Inside the entrenchments, searching wind and numbing cold tortured ill-dressed Southerners. All night the storm held sway, and in the morning wounded men were found frozen to death.

I paid my respects to them and Fort Donelson a century and seven years later almost to the day, and myself complained about the weather, which seemed all too similar. Snow pelted the hilly, forested terrain and winter's bite kept me moving. I wondered aloud that the storm's toll of a century ago wasn't even more dreadful. "Soldiers were pretty tough in those days," replied Don Adams, and his colleague Robert Nelson of Fort Donelson National Military Park's staff added, "They had to be."

Wearing Union blue and Confederate gray, Don and Bob convince today's troops of this. Busloads of Army recruits in basic training at nearby Fort Campbell regularly tour the 600-acre park. They learn that soldiers then often lived in the open and cooked their own food, sometimes went hungry, received poor medical care or none, were flea-bitten and lice-ridden, and endured countless privations above and beyond what we now consider the call of duty.

Fort Campbell's trim new GI's stare as Don and Bob perform the old rifle-musket's strange manual of arms. They watch incredulously as the cumbersome, single-shot weapon is loaded: The task involves almost a dozen different procedures. They perceive that the most adept infantryman could load and fire only a couple of rounds a minute. They grow thoughtful when told that at this stage of the war Blue and Gray sometimes shot at one another from a distance, say, of 150 yards while standing in close ranks—producing a concentrated field of fire and at the same time making easy targets of themselves. When the large, soft lead bullets shattered an arm or leg, surgeons usually amputated.

The Civil War's horrors weighed on generals as well as GI's. U. S. Grant never forgot his soldiers' "absolute suffering" in the brutal cold at Donelson. But all war, to Grant, was suffering, to be ended as quickly as possible by the most direct means. In front of Donelson, heavily reinforced, he wrapped 27,000 men around the perimeter and called on Foote's gunboats to hammer the 15,000 defenders. An attempted Rebel breakout failed. The garrison's two ranking generals, John B. Floyd and Gideon J. Pillow, elected to run rather than surrender. Brig. Gen. Simon B. Buckner, CSA, inherited the unhappy task of asking the Union commander—a good friend since West Point days—for terms.

One bumps squarely into the essential Grant in his plain and simple

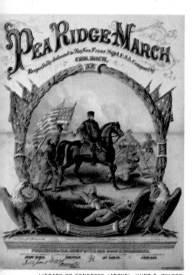

Bursting shell barely misses Rebels at Elkhorn Tavern during the Battle of Pea Ridge, Arkansas, March 7-8. Yanks routed Confederates, ruining the South's plan to carry the war to St. Louis and into Illinois. Sheet music above glorified the struggle that firmed the Union's grip on Missouri and northern Arkansas.

"Tin can on a shingle," *turreted* Monitor *defends grounded* Minnesota *(right) from the* Merrimack *(recommissioned as C.S.S.* Virginia*) at Hampton Roads, Virginia, March 9, 1862. This first duel*

between ironclads ended in a tactical draw but foretold a new era in naval warfare. The Virginia
frustrated Federal plans to send men and matériel up the James to support an attack on Richmond.

reply: "No terms except unconditional and immediate surrender can be accepted. I propose to move immediately upon your works."

This blunt declaration electrified the North, and a hero was born. From this time forward, "Unconditional Surrender" Grant became a byword to the Union, although the general himself received strong abuse on occasion.

For the Confederacy, woe. Right or wrong, as you will, all it was asking was to be left alone. The South's leaders had established a policy of "dispersed defensive": The North would have to do the attacking. Now the North had come. And the North could fight. Union success at Donelson forced the Confederacy to give up Kentucky and much of Tennessee. Nashville, an important supply and transportation center, was evacuated. Mississippi and Alabama presented an inviting target.

Still farther west, an empire beckoned the nation that could secure it—a realm of American states sweeping from sea to shining sea. Untold wealth in gold and silver could pay for a war. For more than a decade thoughtful Southerners had talked of mines worked by slave labor; some had ambitions for conquering Mexican states with their lodes of precious metals. Now, if the Confederacy could hold the California coastline the Union could not possibly enforce a two-ocean blockade... surely the European powers would recognize the new republic....

Enter the adventurous Henry Hopkins Sibley, resigned U. S. Army major, veteran of frontier service, inventor of the field tent and camp stove that keep his name alive. He persuaded President Davis to let him invade New Mexico Territory, where citizens had already voted to seek annexation by the Confederacy. Davis commissioned him brigadier general and told him to go ahead. And Sibley, it appears, held a gossamer dream that California also was ripe for plucking.

In Texas, Sibley assembled a "brigade" armed with squirrel rifles, double-barreled shotguns, lances, and bowie knives. In January 1862, he led more than 2,000 men out of El Paso, proceeded north along the Rio Grande, and on February 21 whipped about 3,800 Union troops, including 11 companies of Regulars, at Valverde. Sibley then advanced to Albuquerque and took it unopposed. A detachment went on to Santa Fe. If the Confederates could take Fort Union in northeast New

Effects of a Confederate infantryman combine the trappings of war and souvenirs of home: knife, photograph, gun, hymnbook, and hardtack—flat, tough biscuits dubbed "sheet-iron crackers" by the troops. On his first campaign, an unseasoned Reb or Yank often carried a clutter of extras. He quickly learned to discard these and keep only the essentials: canteen, pan or tin for cooking, and blanket.

ARNOLD NEWMAN

Great-uncle of the author, Leonidas M. Jordan enlisted in Ohio at age 17. Soon afterward he posed stiffly for an ambrotype — a photographic process that faithfully recorded the subject's image, although in reverse, as one sees himself in a mirror. Affected by the human wreckage of war, the boy wrote his mother: "...if I ever geet home again I will apriciate religious things more."

Mexico they would be well on their way to Denver and the mines.

Colorado raced to its own rescue. After a fantastic forced march, averaging 40 miles a day at one stretch, covering 92 miles in 36 hours in another, cruelly raked by a bitter gale, the men of the 1st Colorado Volunteers tramped into Fort Union. Some had hiked more than 400 miles in 13 days. It amazes me to contemplate that feat, but nothing could halt the "Pike's Peakers." Soon, as a Confederate force moved out of Santa Fe, Colorado's rugged 950-man regiment and other Federal troops stepped south looking for them.

I went looking for both sides on a clear, tangy morning when new snow glistened on high mountain flanks and the living ruts of the old Santa Fe Trail curled beneath them into eternity. North and South had followed the trail to arrive at their rendezvous, treading the same path that Coronado rode more than 300 years earlier in his quest for the fabled riches of Quivira.

In Glorieta Pass, a winding defile below the Sangre de Cristo Range of the Rockies near today's town of Pecos, I caught up with Union and Confederacy. Here they came together on March 28, 1862, and fought for six hours, darting for cover behind rocks big as houses, bushwhacking one another from the shelter of juniper and piñon and cottonwood. The Rebels held the field. Yet the South lost. In a separate action four miles away a force of Federals climbed a mountain, plunged down the other side, and destroyed the Confederate supply train at its foot.

Far into enemy country, caught in barren land without a base of supplies, confronted with increasingly strong opposition, the Confederates found themselves in a hopeless position. From Albuquerque, Sibley commenced a long, agonizing retreat all the way back to Texas. Men collapsed from hunger and thirst and inexorable sun, and wolves ate them. Sibley reached El Paso early in May with the sorry remnant of his brigade strung out behind for fifty miles.

Glorieta Pass: high-water mark of the Confederacy in the West. Jefferson Davis sent Sibley a polite letter acknowledging the "difficulties under which you have labored," wishing for "your continued success."

While the broken Rebels fell back from New Mexico, U. S. Grant, newly a major general, had moved deeper into the South from victory at Fort Donelson. On Sunday morning, April 6, around 37,000 Federals rested near Pittsburg Landing, in Tennessee's far southwest. Another 7,000 camped a few miles north. Within easy marching distance were an additional 20,000 under Brig. Gen. Don Carlos Buell. All had yet to fight a major battle. Only a few had seen any action whatever.

The Confederacy, with equally raw soldiers, determined to halt the invaders then and there. Forty thousand Southerners under the highly touted Albert Sidney Johnston smashed into the bulk of the unwary and divided force at its camp on the Tennessee River by a log meetinghouse called Shiloh Church.

A chaotic struggle ensued. General Johnston, wounded in the leg, bled to death, and the hero of Fort Sumter and Bull Run, Pierre Beauregard, lately transferred to the West, assumed command. That night, Buell's Army of the Ohio arrived. The next day, after hours of savage fighting, the Confederates drew back in retreat.

Men awarded the desperate contest a name to last forever: "Bloody

Pickets trading. Between the lines.

Bitter enemies turn friendly foes long enough to swap tobacco, coffee, and newspapers, a common practice among Blue and Gray pickets. Left, a news correspondent gallops toward the nearest telegraph office. Northern reporters and artists covered the war so thoroughly that Southern generals sometimes learned as much from newspapers as from intelligence reports.

Shiloh." General Grant recalled the carnage more than 20 years later in his memoirs: "I saw an open field, in our possession on the second day, over which the Confederates had made repeated charges the day before, so covered with dead that it would have been possible to walk across the clearing, in any direction, stepping on dead bodies, without a foot touching the ground."

In the greatest battle ever fought on American soil to that time, the Union sustained more than 13,000 casualties and the Confederacy more than 10,000. The amateur armies paid a bitter price for carelessness and poor generalship on both sides. Criticism swirled around Grant's head, and General Halleck, the able administrator who commanded the Army's Department of the Missouri, arrived to take charge in person at Pittsburg Landing. Lincoln, however, responded succinctly to demands for Grant's dismissal: "I can't spare this man; he *fights.*" Another fighter emerged at Shiloh—William T. Sherman, made major general of volunteers for his service there.

Bloody Shiloh opened the South further to the Union. Halleck—ponderous in the field, gingerly beyond normal caution—inched toward Mississippi. Elsewhere, too, grave trouble beset the Confederacy. In northwest Arkansas Union forces won the Battle of Pea Ridge, defeating a hodgepodge of Rebel soldiers that included units of war-whooping Indians: Choctaws, Chickasaws, Cherokees, Creeks, and Seminoles. Many fought with only bows and arrows, tomahawks, and war clubs. That success virtually ended the war in Missouri.

And a long stretch of the Mississippi River came under Union control as the rising Brig. Gen. John Pope occupied Southern strongholds at Island Number Ten and New Madrid, Missouri. In another action 75 miles below New Orleans, Flag Officer David G. Farragut, USN, hurled thousands of shells into Forts Jackson and St. Philip, guarding the Mississippi's channel against invaders, and then slipped past them to capture the South's largest city on April 24. Federals occupied Memphis, Tennessee, 12 days later after a naval battle gave them victory.

Any Confederate hope for a dominion extending from Atlantic to Pacific had died in a lonely New Mexico mountain pass. Now the whole Mississippi Valley was yielding to Union might.

Back in Washington, Abraham Lincoln's patience was sorely tried. Seven months after the fiasco at Bull Run, McClellan still hadn't moved. March arrived. The Confederacy's grotesque ironclad *Virginia* (the revamped U.S.S. *Merrimack*) sank two of the Union's best steam frigates in Hampton Roads. Then the ironclad U.S.S. *Monitor* arrived to fight her rival to a draw. After nearly four hours, *Virginia* retired to the Norfolk navy yard, and the President finally heard some good news clicking in by telegraph from Fort Monroe. If he was delighted, foreign admirals, already building armored vessels of their own, were fascinated as the revolutionary ironclads passed their first test in combat.

The President took another look at McClellan and all he had to do, then removed him as General-in-Chief but retained him in command of the Army of the Potomac. In mid-March, McClellan began ferrying his troops to Fort Monroe, on the tip of Virginia's Peninsula, and Richmond felt the threat of invasion. To cover the enemy's best routes, General Johnston had already evacuated his lines near Centreville and fallen back to strong positions on the Rappahannock and the Rapidan Rivers.

From Fort Monroe the Union army churned along the muddy peninsula to fortified Yorktown, of Revolutionary War renown. Fooled into believing that strong opposition confronted him, when in fact no more than 15,000 Confederates blocked his advance, McClellan began siege operations with about 100,000 men. Johnston, who never had more than 55,000, slipped away after nearly a month; the surprised Federal commander entered Yorktown without a fight. The South had gained precious time, and Johnston was drawing his forces to Richmond.

NEAR THE SLEEPY VILLAGE of Williamsburg the Yankees met Longstreet's hard-fighting infantry, who stood braced in fieldworks. Vicious combat followed. On May 5, advancing toward the disputatious Southerners in driving rain, a Union skirmisher plunged into hell:

"They immediately opened fire upon us ... from the fort, while from their rifle-pits came a hum of bullets and crackle of musketry. Their heavy shot came crashing among the tangled abatis of fallen timber, and plowed up the dirt in our front, rebounding and tearing through the branches of the woods in our rear. The constant hissing of the bullets, with their sharp *ping* or *bizz* whispering around and sometimes into us, gave me a sickening feeling ... and a sort of faintness.... The little rifle-pits in our front fairly blazed with musketry, and the continuous *snap, snap, crack, crack* was murderous."

The delaying action permitted Johnston's successful withdrawal, though heavy rain had turned roads into thick bogs of mud. Retreating along Williamsburg's Duke of Gloucester Street—where George Washington, Thomas Jefferson, George Mason, and Patrick Henry had ridden in an earlier, better day—the Confederacy's soggy legions made only one mile an hour through the knee-deep mire, and McClellan's pace toward Richmond was little better.

Who remembers now? Not my wife Jane, who spent her undergraduate years at the College of William and Mary there. Not most of the good people who reside there today, immersed as they are in colonial history. Not most Virginians who live near the earthworks that still cross the peninsula in an irregular line: Surely *those* aren't redoubts from which Rebel fire flashed—only little hills, clogged with trees and brush; *that* can't be Fort Magruder, where Union Brig. Gen. Joseph Hooker's assault was sternly repulsed—merely an overgrown embankment to use as a target for empty beer cans.

The affair at Williamsburg, like the contest at Champion Hill, finds few spectators in our time. Yet it tantalizes me, fascinated watcher of the war. What, I ask myself, if the careful McClellan had caught up with Joe Johnston there and thrashed him? Could anything have stopped "Little Mac" from marching into Richmond, bringing the conflict to an early end? Might not his chances of the Presidency have been stronger when, in 1864, he ran against Lincoln? *President* McClellan...?

So much for conjecture. Might-have-beens strew the conflict's wake. The fact is that Williamsburg's Civil War story lives on, if one searches. It reached out and tugged at Jane and me one day in the guise of a pleasant, gray-haired gentlewoman named Elizabeth Lee Henderson, a lifelong resident like her people before her and theirs before them. We

Solitary Confederate picket mirrors the hardship of war in winter. Men charged with picket duty stood stints as early-warning attack sentries for units quartered nearby. By 1862 the rigors of army life—ragged clothing, improper diet, filth, and disease—plagued troops. "I wish ... I was home by my own fireside.... A Soldiers life ... is not what it is cracked up to be," wrote a disenchanted Reb.
JULIAN SCOTT, 1899, COURTESY BEVERLY DUBOSE

sat in Mrs. Henderson's parlor, beside Duke of Gloucester Street, and she spoke of her grandmother, Victoria King.

Victoria was a dark-haired snippet of 16, said Mrs. Henderson, when Union soldiers occupied Williamsburg. The Baptist Church, turned into a hospital, sheltered many wounded Confederates, and every day Victoria carried biscuits and buttermilk and the like to them.

"She walked right past this house where we're sitting now," said Mrs. Henderson. "She wore a sunbonnet and a calico hoopskirt, and she never used the sidewalk because of the Union flags hanging over it. The Yankees posted a guard to make townsfolk pass under the Stars and Stripes. When Grandmother approached, he motioned to her. She took

Yawning Yanks fall out for morning roll call. A drummer boy warms his hands with his breath after beating out Reveille in the wintry dawn. Conical Sibley tents housed a stove and a score of soldiers who slept spoon fashion. When one cried "Spoon!" all of the men would roll over on their other side.

a crock of buttermilk, hit him over the head with it, and knocked him down. Then she went back to Wetherburn's tavern, got more buttermilk, and marched up the street past the dazed guard. Never from that time on did anybody bother her."

Jane and I were captivated. With spirit like that, the best of the Old South should live forever. Perhaps, in a way, it will. Did I fancy a twinkle in Mrs. Henderson's eye? Was there something of her indomitable kinsman, Robert E. Lee, in Mrs. Henderson's quiet, warm dignity?

"Victoria was a spitfire!" she continued. "They called her 'the lovely little Rebel.' She married Edward Lee, who was related to Robert, and lived to be 99. Not long before Grandmother died, World War II broke out. When I told her, she said: 'What! The Yankees again?' "

For the Confederacy, as spring blended into summer in 1862, it had been pretty much the Yankees' year all round. Down in Georgia, a daring raid by Federals in civilian clothes drove newspapers to a frenzy of superlatives. The *Southern Confederacy* of April 15 proclaimed the amazing story in stentorian headlines: "The Great Railroad Chase!— THE MOST EXTRAORDINARY AND ASTOUNDING ADVENTURE OF THE WAR!! —The Most Daring Undertaking That Yankees Ever Planned Or Attempted To Execute!"

A party of soldiers and a civilian spy, all Ohioans clad in mufti, had infiltrated northwest Georgia intending to cut the rail line and sever communications between Atlanta and Chattanooga. On a rainy day at Big Shanty (now Kennesaw), where the locomotive "General" had halted for a breakfast stop, they uncoupled the train's passenger cars and careened northwest, pulling three boxcars. Soon, in angry pursuit roared Confederates aboard the "Texas," running backward.

After a 90-mile dash unparalleled in railroading history, a headlong chase of monster after monster, the Yankees ran out of fuel. Abandoning the pirated locomotive, they fled into woods. The raiders were captured within a couple of days after the story appeared. Eight were put to death as spies in Atlanta, eight others escaped successfully from prison, and six were released in a prisoner exchange within a year.

Little came of it all except that the Medal of Honor was awarded for the first time to the audacious band's soldiers. One recipient, identity unknown, detracts from the glory of his comrades, though I think understandably. After 150 lashes, according to a newly discovered letter I saw in the Georgia Department of Archives and History in Atlanta, a captured raider revealed all he knew about the raid and his still-missing comrades.

The South hadn't quit muttering about the great railroad chase when Maj. Gen. Benjamin Franklin Butler, military governor of New Orleans, triggered a towering volcano of Confederate wrath. Charles L. Dufour, chronicler of the city's capture, instructor in history at Tulane University, and newspaper columnist, told Jane and me about it as we paused at the old United States Mint.

The martinet Butler, Mr. Dufour said, had angered the populace in many ways. Some hot-blooded citizens, including women, openly sneered at Union officers and men, vilified them, spat on them, dumped garbage on their heads from second-story windows, and what not.

Mustachios quivering, the walrus-like Butler took action with his

First Day

Union Encampments △△△

First Attack
Second Attack
Last Attack
Defensive Lines ⊏⊐⊐⊐⊐
Reinforcements →

Retreat - - →
Artillery ↓↓↓↓↓

Second Day

First Attack
Last Attack
Initial Lines, A.M. ━ ━ ━ ━

Retreat - - - →
Union Forces ■
Confederate Forces ■

As spring comes on, the Confederacy seeks to counter Union gains in the West. With the Mississippi Valley at stake, *Johnston* masses troops at Corinth, Mississippi, a vital rail center. He decides to strike Grant and Buell separately in southwest Tennessee before they can combine. On April 6 at dawn 40,000 Rebels suddenly hit Grant's force of about equal size encamped in a line extending from Sherman's division around Shiloh Church (A)

Italics Denote Confederate Officers

to Prentiss' left (B) and Stuart's camp (C). The raw troops fight stubbornly, a chaotic battle raging around the Peach Orchard (D) and Bloody Pond to the Hornet's Nest (E). Stuart is driven toward Pittsburg Landing (F); McClernand takes the brunt of battle for Sherman's broken division, falling back across Tillman's Hollow (G). Prentiss holds the Hornet's Nest until surrounded. *Johnston* falls. Both sides lose order but not heart. By late afternoon the Federals struggle to save the landing as steamers bring up Buell's men. After a last attack on the Union line (H), the Rebels, beaten back, retire to regroup. At dawn Grant—reinforced by Lew Wallace's division (I)—and Buell attack from their imperiled line (J,K,L) and push the startled enemy back over the battlefield. In midafternoon *Beauregard* orders a retreat; his tired and shaken men withdraw (M) to Corinth, 25 miles to the south.

"Woman Order" of May 15: "Any Female" insulting any man in Federal uniform might be "treated as a woman of the town plying her avocation."

My wife gasped. "What a despicable thing to do," she exclaimed.

"I'm no admirer of Ben Butler," replied our host softly. "But the ladies of New Orleans weren't behaving like ladies. What Butler really said was, 'if you don't behave like a lady, you can't expect to be treated like one.' And the insults stopped. On that count, I don't think Butler really deserved the abuse that followed, but he surely caught it. His order even roused condemnation in Parliament."

People called him "Beast Butler." Later President Davis outlawed him and directed that he be hanged without trial if captured. The pastor of St. Patrick's Catholic Church, Father James Mullon, handled Butler nicely, I think. As we drove past the old church, Mr. Dufour recalled that the general had accused the peppery priest, a stanch Confederate, of refusing to bury a Union soldier. Father Mullon shot back, "I'm ready to bury the whole Union army!"

THE CONFEDERACY'S FORTUNES turned for the better as June arrived. True, General McClellan now camped in front of Richmond with 105,000 fighting men, his infantry as close as eight miles to the Capitol itself. But General Johnston attacked him there in the Battle of Seven Pines (Fair Oaks), and McClellan bogged down after the inconclusive engagement—or perhaps his technique, polite strangulation, only made it seem so. Greatly overestimating his foe's strength, as at Yorktown, he threw up breastworks and settled in, begging Lincoln for more troops the while.

The general's troubles were only beginning. Unhappily for him, and the Union, Johnston had been severely wounded at Seven Pines, and Robert E. Lee succeeded him. That gentleman would take the raggle-taggle Army of Northern Virginia and mold it in the image of his own devotion to the South's cause, and the North would have a fight on its hands all the way to an April day three years later at an obscure village called Appomattox Court House.

Lincoln had not sent reinforcements enough to suit McClellan. Stonewall Jackson and his evanescent "foot cavalry" had seen to that, creating a diversion in the Shenandoah Valley that tied up more than 60,000 Union troops and drove Washington frantic with fear of invasion.

Military historians look on Jackson's Valley Campaign as one of the most brilliant in warfare's annals. Between March 23 and June 9, with 4,200 iron-legged riflemen at first and 17,000 at most, he marched 676 miles, skirmished almost daily, fought five pitched battles, and perplexed men from three Union commands who were trying to catch him.

In all the war, nobody came any odder than Thomas J. Jackson. An 1846 graduate of West Point, he won two brevets for distinguished service in the Mexican War and left the Army in 1851 to teach at the Virginia Military Institute. A Presbyterian deacon, Jackson formed Sunday School classes for Negroes, opposed the idea of civil war, and neither smoked, drank, nor played cards. He ate sparingly and often called for lemons, on which he liked to suck.

Jackson disliked to break the Sabbath by fighting, but believed his cause a righteous one. He often lifted his face to the Heavens, whence

JAMES P. BLAIR (ABOVE); LIBRARY OF CONGRESS

cometh all help. Once, worrying aloud that captured wagon stores might be fallen upon by the enemy, he interrupted himself frequently in silent prayer. "The men," recalled one of his generals, Richard Taylor, only son of former President Zachary Taylor, "said that his anxiety about the wagons was because of the lemons among the stores."

Daring and resourceful, striking mightily when his foes least expected him, Jackson coursed between the Blue Ridge and the Appalachians like a dark-bearded Joshua, strange light filling his piercing blue eyes in the blaze of battle. "He lives by the New Testament and fights by the Old," says Douglas Southall Freeman, the great biographer of Lee and his lieutenants.

Maj. Gen. Nathaniel P. Banks, one of many Union politicians given high rank to lead the great new volunteer armies, headed the initial Federal force sent to guard the Valley. The wily Rebel outwitted him again and again, and it all seemed rather dull to a young soldier in Banks's command:

"Ther is nothing of interest going on at present," he wrote home. "We have got so uste to the canons that we hartly notice it we have noth to do except to run after the rebels . . . our regiment is on picket today and I was left to cok the rations for our mess I will have to take them out somethin to eat be fore long . . ."

My great-uncle, Pvt. Leonidas Jordan, a 17-year-old farm boy from Roseville, Ohio, penned those words on April 6, 1862, at a rain-sodden camp near Woodstock, Virginia. Several of his letters have come down to me, and I am proud to have them. Written in a strong, clear hand, full of misspellings and empty of punctuation, they reveal a plain American's faith in his country and his devotion to home and family.

The Civil War belonged to the soldiers, as Grant, Lee, and Jackson knew well, and the average soldier of both sides was a farm boy. He

Lt. Gen. Albert Sidney Johnston died on April 6 at Shiloh trying to destroy Grant's army in Tennessee. Some 23,000 casualties occurred in two days as Rebels strove futilely to stem the Union's western invasion of the Confederacy. Shiloh's thirsting wounded crawled to the pond above, staining it red as they drank. Ever after it bore the name "Bloody Pond."

took a good look at the land he traveled over, and appraised its crops and livestock with a keen eye; the subject of food was especially dear to him now.

Imbued with the free spirit of the outdoors, he didn't care much about discipline (sometimes he didn't care at all). A plain American, the average recruit was unsophisticated but quick to learn; the temptations of camp life usually were available and concupiscence sometimes got the upper hand; he was of the earth, and earthy. Like his forefathers, he fought as a citizen bearing arms. And he was God-fearing. Generally he could die in peace because he knew, deep inside, that he had done his duty and was going to a better place. He had faith.

Some sense of this comes through in a note added to Leonidas Jordan's letter by his hometown buddy, J. J. Hitchcock:

"Dear friends i will give you a few lines to let you no that i am still alive and well with the exception of a bad cold which we are all liable to have at home as well as here we have a verry good time chasing old Jackson so far . . . we have run him a bout forty five miles over a verry nice turnpike we give them a few pills once and a while to keep them regular i dont think we will move from here till we are paid off we will then send our money home if we can get any safe way to send it . . ."

Civil War soldiers sent home a pitifully small amount. The most a Union infantry private ever received was $16 a month; top pay for his Southern counterpart amounted to an inflation-shriveled $18. Northern soldiers also ate better than Confederates, who rarely obtained sufficient food. Billy Yank's staples consisted of bread, meat, dried vegetables, and coffee; Johnny Reb mostly ate corn bread, and salt or pickled beef and pork. He couldn't get coffee because of the blockade.

The Federal's cracker ration broke his teeth and turned his stomach, but he couldn't do without it. He called it "hardtack," when not disposed to call it worse. A flour-and-water biscuit roughly three inches square and half an inch thick, hardtack often was inhabited by weevils. Dunking

Racing in reverse, Rebel engine "Texas" pursues Union raiders during an exploit known as "The Great Locomotive Chase." The Federals had stolen a Chattanooga-bound engine in Georgia, April 12, 1862, intending to destroy railroad bridges and leave the Tennessee city an isolated target for attack. Their complicated plot miscarried but dramatized the importance of railroads in the Civil War. Map below compares the relative strength of Northern and Southern train systems. Of 31,000-odd miles of rails in the Nation at the war's outbreak, only about 9,000 served the Confederacy.

WILBUR G. KURTZ, 1965, COURTESY COL. JAMES G. BOGLE, USA (RET.)

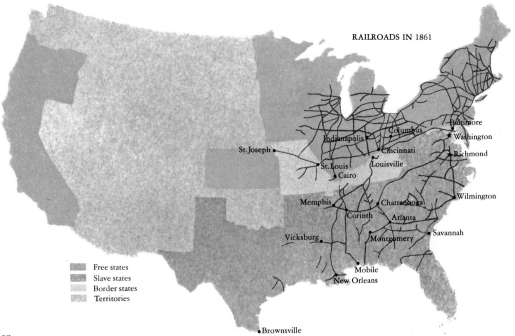

RAILROADS IN 1861

Free states
Slave states
Border states
Territories

Baltimore
Washington
Columbus
Indianapolis
Cincinnati
St. Joseph
Richmond
St. Louis
Louisville
Cairo
Wilmington
Memphis
Chattanooga
Corinth
Atlanta
Vicksburg
Montgomery
Savannah
Mobile
New Orleans

Brownsville

Shower of mortar shells rains on star-shaped Fort Jackson on the Mississippi River's west bank as Union ships battle upstream past the key ramparts defending New Orleans, April 24. Moored at Fort St. Philip on the opposite bank, the unfinished and immobile Rebel ironclad Louisiana *(left foreground) blasts at* Hartford, *the ship of Flag Officer David G. Farragut. One Federal officer described*

the predawn engagement as "the breaking up of the universe with the moon and all the stars bursting in our midst." With surprisingly few casualties, Farragut succeeded in running the forts and on April 25 steamed into the harbor of New Orleans. His victory put the Confederacy's greatest port and largest city in Union hands, providing a southern base for the Federal drive to control the Mississippi.

a biscuit in coffee brought the weevils to the surface, where they could be skimmed off. Some men preferred to eat hardtack in the dark.

Ten of these crackers might make up a day's bread ration in the field. Their iron consistency challenged ingenuity and provided an unending source of discussion. Smashed into crumbs by a rifle butt, they often fortified stews. Fried in bacon drippings, they tended not to distress the teeth. One day a Kansan overheard this dialogue:

Sergeant: "Boys I was eating a piece of hardtack this morning, and I bit on something soft; what do you think it was?"

Private: "A worm?"

Sergeant: "No by G-d, it was a ten penny nail."

My great-uncle may not actually have *liked* hardtack, which he termed "as hard as a poplar chip," but he too made his peace with it. "We pound cracers up wright fine and make mush out of bean soup," he once informed his sister Mary. "... wont you come over and have some...."

I guess young Private Jordan needed all the food he could get; he wasn't very big and dealing with General Jackson was rugged work. Gray-eyed and dark-haired, he stood only 5 feet 6 inches tall. He told his parents of marches that lasted from 1 a.m. to 8 p.m. and started again the next morning. The rifle-musket he shouldered weighed about 10 pounds. He spoke of wading a swift river, waist-deep: "It was amising to see to or thre hunared men in the water some stumbled and fell and went sailing down the river...." And he knew another enemy, too: "We have lost one of our best men he died of the tyaphoit fever...."

On May 4, he wrote that his regiment, the 62nd Ohio, had marched 16 miles the previous day. "We no nothing of Jackson," he added. "I am geting tired of chasing him but mabe we will get him cornered some of these days ... the people are geting tired of this war they say they cant whip us ... I would like to be at home now it looks like I ot be at work at somthing useful the people around her have no chance to put in a crop their horses all bing pressed in the sarvice of the rebels...."

I do not know from Private Jordan what happened to him after that, for his letters ceased. I know from my resourceful friends at the

Southern broadside answers the "Woman Order" issued by Maj. Gen. Benjamin F. Butler, despised military governor of New Orleans after Farragut took the city. Butler's method of forcing Rebel women to respect U. S. occupation troops worked but raised indignation in the Confederacy and even abroad. In the sketch (right), artist Adalbert John Volck portrays a despotic Butler protecting the ignorant and the wicked while urging the oppression of the virtuous.

BUTLER'S PROCLAMATION

An outrageous insult to the Women of New Orleans!

Southern Men, avenge their wrongs !!!

Head-Quarters, Department of the Gulf,
New Orleans, May 15, 1862.

General Orders, No. 28.

As the Officers and Soldiers of the United States have been subject to repeated insults from the women calling themselves ladies of New Orleans, in return for the most scrupulous non-interference and courtesy on our part, it is ordered that hereafter when any Female shall, by word, gesture, or movement, insult or show contempt for any officer or soldier of the United States, she shall be regarded and held liable to be treated as a woman of the town plying her avocation.

By command of Maj.-Gen. BUTLER,
GEORGE C. STRONG,
A. A. G. Chief of Stables

National Archives in Washington. On May 24, Union records show, he was admitted to a field hospital at the town of Strasburg, stricken by typhoid fever. The hospital register noted that he was "some better."

That same morning, General Banks, feeling secure in his fortifications at Strasburg, discovered to his anguish that Jackson's army had slipped up on his flank. He ordered a retreat and didn't really stop until, in confusion and disorder, he fled across the Potomac into Maryland.

Left behind, Leonidas was captured. Prisoners with typhoid, however, were less than desirable, and he received a parole. Somehow the boy made his way home to Ohio. On July 23, at Columbus, he received a medical discharge from the army. "In all probability," noted the examining physician in cold medical appraisal, "he will never be fit to perform the duties devolving on a soldier." The doctor was wrong. We shall meet Private Jordan again, on a field in Georgia.

Poor McClellan. He fidgeted on Richmond's eastern outskirts, asking for reinforcements, while Lee began ringing the city with entrenchments and his disgruntled, shovel-wielding troops styled him "King of Spades." Lee understood his opponent's strategy and declined to sit still for it. He needed information; and brash Jeb Stuart, in a spectacular three-day ride, took his cavalry completely around the Federal army, outdistancing pursuing horsemen under Brig. Gen. Philip St. George Cooke—his father-in-law. Richmond's morale leaped, and Washington suffered another large pain.

Most important of all, Stuart had found McClellan's right flank in the air—completely open to attack. Lee promptly ordered Stonewall Jackson to bring his light-traveling veterans of the Valley to strike at that opening. They set off quickly: a lean and shaggy wolfpack with blanket rolls slung over shoulders, frying-pan handles stuck in gun barrels, and tin cups dangling from belts. When they arrived, Lee had about 85,000 fighting men, the largest force he would ever command, and he proposed to drive McClellan and his 105,000 away from the city's gates.

Late in June, from the hot, humid lowlands and swamps outside the Capital, at last resounded the wild symphony of war—musketry's monotonous rattle swelling to a steady metallic threnody; artillery's sudden *whir-r-r* providing the counterpoint of a locomotive in full flight, screams of wounded men a ragged chorus to it all.

For a week the fight swirled on through forests and fields and malarial bogs, while Richmond and Washington waited and the god of battles dispensed fame to strange-sounding things and places: to the Chickahominy River, and a crossroads called Mechanicsville; to Gaines's Mill, and Savage Station on the Richmond and York River Railroad; to White Oak Swamp, and Malvern Hill, where Union canister, case shot, and shell struck down more than half of the South's 5,000-odd casualties.

People called it *the* Seven Days after July 1, when it was over, and Richmond relaxed, safe. Lee had driven McClellan and the Army of the Potomac back 18 miles from the city to their new, well-fortified base at Harrison's Landing on the James River. Now there would be no quick end to the war, which Lee desired as much as Lincoln. "Under ordinary circumstances," the Confederate general wrote, "the Federal Army should have been destroyed." As a major cause of its escape he cited "the want of correct and timely information."

The want of correct and timely information shackled leaders through-out the Civil War, altering its course countless times. I marvel, watching a harried commander scribble orders to attack and basing them on inadequate knowledge of terrain and enemy, watching a courier gallop off with the orders toward a distant brigadier whose situation will change completely while horse and rider are en route — I marvel, not at the horrible confusion of the battles, but at the officers and men who fought so bravely and earnestly under such circumstances.

AFTER THE SEVEN DAYS, Lincoln made another attempt to end his army's confusion and brought Halleck from the west as General-in-Chief. U. S. Grant succeeded Halleck. Loud-mouthed General Pope, hero of the Mississippi Valley, also came east to assemble dispersed Federal forces in northern Virginia for an overland march on Richmond.

Pope meant well, but announced his intentions badly; fellow officers considered him a "bag of wind." Addressing his new command, he declared that soldiers in the West always saw "the backs of our enemies"; now this would become the Eastern soldiers' agreeable lot. The story went around that he bragged his headquarters would be in the saddle. That, snorted critics, was where his hindquarters ought to be.

Robert E. Lee obviously had to try to keep Pope from linking up with McClellan, still resting at Harrison's Landing. Lee dispatched Stonewall Jackson north to meet the new invading army led by the hero of the West. Gray and Blue tangled at Cedar Mountain, and on August 14 the Army of the Potomac began embarking from Newport News to come to Pope's aid. With the campaign mounting, Lee took the field.

Near the old battleground at Bull Run, as August ended, with most of McClellan's men now reaching his command, it was Pope's turn to lack correct and timely information. Thoroughly confused, he groped after Jackson's corps, unaware that another Confederate corps under Longstreet had come up. Lee suggested three times to Longstreet that he strike the unsuspecting Pope on the left flank. When Longstreet finally committed his 30,000 men, Pope suffered a crushing defeat.

Again Northerners retired ignominiously upon Washington from Bull Run. Just two months earlier, Lee had driven one invading army from Richmond; now he had smashed another. Both times he had been badly outnumbered. In Virginia, the war was back where it started.

Pope was relieved and sent west. Lincoln gave the Army of the Potomac back to McClellan despite bitter opposition within his Cabinet. The army remained devoted to McClellan. No one else could remake it and instill it with esprit, Lincoln was sure, and he was right. McClellan promptly worked his old magic and a rejuvenated command took shape.

The President worried about Rebel gains in Tennessee and Kentucky, worried about the very real possibility that Britain and France would recognize the Confederacy as a nation, worried about Lee's ever-dangerous Army of Northern Virginia. *Continued on page 104*

Stonewall Jackson gazes into the Shenandoah Valley, scene of his brilliant campaign in the spring of 1862. Menacing Washington, D. C., with his maneuvers, the wily general prevented reinforcements from joining the Union army then massing for an attack on Richmond, and gave Lee a chance to save the city.

N. C. WYETH, 1910, M. KNOEDLER & CO.

Fording a tributary of Virginia's Chickahominy River, June 29, the Army of the Potomac withdraws after a frustrated

attempt to take the Rebel Capital. In orderly retreat, the Federals saved themselves by fending off Lee's flanking attacks.

Maj. Gen. George B. McClellan's overly cautious direction of the Peninsular Campaign, March-July 1862, cost him the opportunity to capture Richmond and shorten the war. "Little Mac" (right) moved the Army of the Potomac by ship to Fort Monroe at the tip of the Virginia Peninsula. Then he advanced to within a few miles of Richmond with such deliberation the Rebels had a chance to prepare for an effective attack. The outcome: a Union retreat during the clashes known as the Seven Days' Battles. At left, Confederates fire at a balloon manned by Professor T. S. C. Lowe, who observed enemy positions and telegraphed his reports to Federal commanders.

At Malvern Hill—perfect ground for a fortress in the field—Federal artillery dominates the last battle of the Seven Days. In the tangled swamps of the Chickahominy, McClellan has managed to stand off *Lee* and to change his base from an endangered site on the Pamunkey River to a safer one on the James. Now, as his great supply train gets to the river and the protection of Union gunboats, he places his guns (A) and infantry on this open plateau, where cleared ground gives them an ideal field of fire. On the hot windless morning of July 1, *Lee* struggles to concentrate his army, hampered by an inexperienced staff with only one map available, new officers replacing the disabled, everyone strained by prolonged combat. As he deploys his forces, his batteries (B) begin firing about 1 p.m. The Federals soon overpower them with field artillery, heavy siege guns at the Malvern House (C), and supporting fire from their gunboats. In midafternoon Southern divisions begin a series of disjointed infantry attacks. *Magruder* sends forward 5,000 men (D) toward the Crew House; *D. H. Hill*'s division tries the eastern end of the slope (E); *Stonewall Jack-*

To Harrison's Landing

N

C

A

Quaker Road

A

Poindexter
House

West
House

A

A

River Road

A

A

B

E

Crew House

E

F

D

Willis Church Road

B

Union Forces

Confederate Forces

Skirmishers ─ ─ ─ ─ ─

Lines

Attack

Artillery ↓↓↓↓↓↓↓↓

Long Bridge Road   To Richmond

0   1/2

STATUTE MILE

Richard Schlecht

son fails to turn the right flank, other units
assail the steep bluffs to the west (F). Federal guns sweep the open ground and
secure the victory—with about 5,000 victims. Not war, said *Hill:* "It was murder."
That night the Army of the Potomac reaches Harrison's Landing on the river; a
downpour the next day balks *Lee*'s effort
to make yet another attack. Still, he has
foiled the Union's first great blow against
the Capital of the Confederate States. He
will smash the Federals in a second battle
at Bull Run, then take the war to the North,
always outnumbered, always audacious.

For General Lee had forded the Potomac and invaded the North—thousands of his men shoeless, all of them weary from their labors at Second Manassas, and all convinced that under Lee they were invincible.

Lee marched north for several reasons. He meant to keep the initiative, and to give bloodstained Virginia a respite from war. He needed food for men and horses. He hoped that the people of border-state Maryland would flock to the South's cause. Too, the chorus of antiwar sentiment in the North should swell; Europe would be strongly impressed; the Confederacy would win her independence—and peace.

It was not to be. A mislaid copy of Lee's orders had fallen into McClellan's hands. For once, he moved. He set out after the invaders. Had he moved faster, he would have crushed Lee, who had divided his army in order to capture Harper's Ferry and about 12,000 Yankees there.

L EE TURNED at bay near a town called Sharpsburg, on the banks of Antietam Creek hard by the Potomac River. When McClellan finally struck, as night's blackness yielded to dawn on September 17, Lee's forces were rapidly coming together. The war hung in the balance.

It amounted to three separate battles, each desperate, and the bloodletting lasted until dusk. "The lanterns of the ambulance corps on both sides were soon flickering like the fireflies on a Southern river," writes Douglas Southall Freeman, "but they did not reach all the corners of the fields or penetrate the shadows in the woods and under the rocks where the dead stiffened and the wounded cried in vain for water."

Lee took 40,000 men to Sharpsburg, and they repulsed five major assaults as McClellan used about half of his 87,000 troops. The Battle of Antietam lives in memory as the Civil War's bloodiest day: About 12,000 Northerners fell there, and more than 10,500 Southerners.

Next day, Lee, knowing his shattered forces could not take the offensive, waited for any attack McClellan might make. Late that night the Army of Northern Virginia, unmolested, recrossed the Potomac for home. McClellan made little effort to bother the retreating foe. As a veteran wrote later, McClellan "always saw double when he looked Rebelward." He had won—and wasted—a victory.

Yet it proved a particular boon to Lincoln, who needed a dramatic occasion to announce a plan he had entertained for weeks. On September 22 he called the Cabinet together. Salmon P. Chase, Secretary of the Treasury, kept a record: "'. . . The action of the army against the rebels has not been quite what I should have best liked,' said the President. 'But they have been driven out of Maryland, and Pennsylvania is no longer in danger of invasion. When the rebel army was at Frederick, I determined, as soon as it should be driven out of Maryland, to issue a Proclamation of Emancipation such as I thought most likely to be useful. I said nothing to anyone; but I made the promise to myself, and (hesitating a little)—to my Maker. The rebel army is now driven out, and I am going to fulfill that promise. . . .'"

That same day Lincoln issued the preliminary Emancipation Proclamation. A warning, it served notice to the South that as of January 1, 1863, all slaves within any state or district in rebellion against the United States ". . . shall be then, thenceforward, and forever free." To the cry of "Preserve the Union" Lincoln added the issue of human liberty. Thus

Federal reserves pause en route to Sharpsburg, Maryland, where McClellan failed to use them against Lee. Lifeless Rebels (be-

104

low left) testify to the high cost of Lee's northern invasion, a move to carry the war to the enemy and perhaps gain recognition from France and Britain. At Antietam Creek, McClellan forced Lee to retreat but did not pursue him. Seven weeks later, Lincoln relieved the reluctant general of his command. Bloody Lane (below right), today a shrine, got its name on the war's most sanguinary day, September 17, 1862.

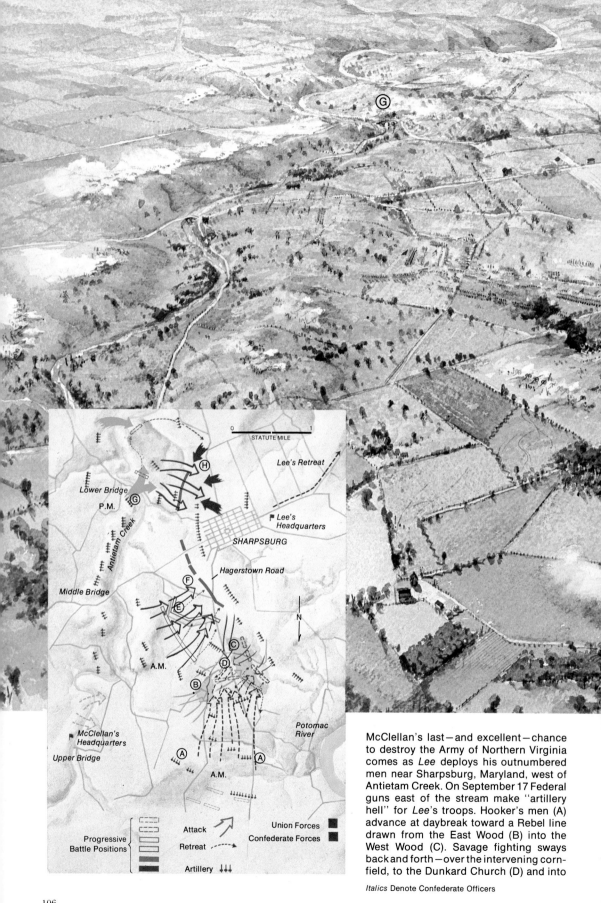

0
1
STATUTE MILE

Lee's Retreat

Lee's
Headquarters

SHARPSBURG

Hagerstown Road

Lower Bridge

P.M.

Antietam Creek

Middle Bridge

N

McClellan's
Headquarters

Upper Bridge

A.M.

Potomac
River

A.M.

Progressive
Battle Positions

Attack

Retreat

Artillery

Union Forces
Confederate Forces

McClellan's last—and excellent—chance
to destroy the Army of Northern Virginia
comes as *Lee* deploys his outnumbered
men near Sharpsburg, Maryland, west of
Antietam Creek. On September 17 Federal
guns east of the stream make "artillery
hell" for *Lee*'s troops. Hooker's men (A)
advance at daybreak toward a Rebel line
drawn from the East Wood (B) into the
West Wood (C). Savage fighting sways
back and forth—over the intervening corn-
field, to the Dunkard Church (D) and into

Italics Denote Confederate Officers

the West Wood—till both sides are virtually fought out by 10 a.m. Fresh Federals arrive by the upper bridge and nearby fords. They attack past the burning Roulette and Mumma farmhouses (center), only to be halted at Sunken Road (Bloody Lane) (E), for several murderous hours. They drive past the Piper House (F), finally stopping before the tattered center of the Confederate line; the attack that would crush it never comes. In early afternoon Burnside's men belatedly cross the lower bridge (G) after others wade fords to the south. This third uncoordinated major action meets a last-minute check (H) from *A. P. Hill*'s "Light Division," rushing in from Harper's Ferry. All day *Lee* steadily shifts men and guns to cope with each emergency. McClellan, convinced that he faces a vastly superior foe, holds back his strong reserves. The next day *Lee*'s mauled army braces for battle, then slips away unmolested—taking with it the Union hope of conclusive victory in the East.

he not only answered demands for a war against slavery, he ended the likelihood of foreign intervention for the Confederacy. Englishmen and Frenchmen could never embrace a nation based on slavery.

That was that, but it did nothing about getting on with the war. With the Army of the Potomac resting in Maryland, Lincoln paid a visit. Surveying the encampment's white tents dotting the rolling, golden countryside, the President turned to a friend and asked: "Do you know what this is?"

Surprised, the friend replied: "It is the Army of the Potomac."

Lincoln had him. "So it is called, but that is a mistake; it is only McClellan's bodyguard."

O N OCTOBER 6, the President could take it no longer. General-in-Chief Halleck telegraphed McClellan: "The President directs that you cross the Potomac and give battle to the enemy or drive him south. . . ." Yet even this did not budge McClellan, and a few days later the Confederacy's beplumed Jeb Stuart and 1,800 cavalrymen raided Chambersburg, Pennsylvania, and then dashed contemptuously around the Army of the Potomac for a second time.

At length McClellan set his faithful army stepping into Virginia, but Lincoln's patience had run out. On November 5, he relieved McClellan and turned command of the Army of the Potomac over to Maj. Gen. Ambrose E. Burnside, whose luxuriant muttonchop whiskers still give him fame. A likeable, impressive six-footer, West Pointer Burnside knew his limitations; it is a pity Lincoln didn't take him at his word. "I am not competent to command such a large army," he said, and proved it tragically.

At Fredericksburg, on a raw day in mid-December, Burnside put brave soldiers across the Rappahannock River and stormed Lee precisely where he hoped they would—in an impregnable position on heights above the town. Six grand and hopeless Union assaults were hurled back before nightfall ended the slaughter.

Lee watched it all: smoke and dust and din of battle, fiendish yipping of the Rebel yell, mounted officers shouting orders, human waves of death in ebb and flow. Turning to Longstreet, he said, "It is well that war is so terrible—we should grow too fond of it."

But the wounded say it their own way. They scream and groan and curse as they writhe toward the rear, those who can move. They cry out for water, too, and sometimes they find succor.

At Fredericksburg, young Sgt. Richard Kirkland of the 2nd South Carolina could not stand the piteous appeals. He walked head up into that no-man's-land, expecting a Yankee sharpshooter's bullet. None came, and he gave water to the nearest wounded Federal, and the next, and the next. Many times he returned for water in the following hour and a half. He did not stop until he had ministered to every wounded man on his part of the front.

Burnside offered battle no more, and Lee chose not to attack. The Federals drew back, and war in the East was over for the time being. Winter again took command. To Union and Confederacy alike, 1862's vicious testing and waste made one thing supremely clear: There would be more. Much more.

Confederate sharpshooters snipe at Federal engineers laying a pontoon bridge across the Rappahannock River for Gen. Ambrose E. Burn-

side's attack on Lee at Fredericksburg. Diorama (below left) shows buildings damaged by artillery fire as Union troops set forth to assault an impregnable Confederate position on Marye's Heights, December 13. Rebels mowed down waves of dauntless men, and Burnside withdrew. Below right: Fredericksburg spires stand as they did in 1862 when Lee once again halted a Federal advance on Richmond.

1863:
WAR STALKS THE LAND

CHAPTER FOUR

ONE DAY EARLY IN 1863 as the shivering antagonists stared at one another across the narrow Rappahannock, a Union band appeared at riverside and serenaded the startled Southern camp with Northern tunes. It was better than no music at all, but the nearest Rebel listeners, ragamuffins on picket, shouted for their own songs. Immediately the band struck up the lilting bars of "Dixie," "Maryland, My Maryland," "The Bonnie Blue Flag," and a heartfelt cheer rose from Confederate throats. Then, after a moment of silence like the hush before an amen, the band sent forth the sweet, sad notes of "Home, Sweet Home." Men on both sides of the river shouted in joy as the music died away, and tears filled many a veteran's eyes.

Love of home could unite those estranged Americans; that is what they were fighting for, mostly. So could misery; that is what they were fighting against, right then. Scurvy cut soldiers down that bleak, snowy winter. For a time Federal troops ate nothing but salt pork and hardtack. Confederates fared so poorly that General Lee appealed to Richmond. "Their ration," he wrote, "...consists of one-fourth pound of bacon, 18 ounces of flour, 10 pounds of rice to each 100 men about every third day, with some few peas and a small amount of dried fruit occasionally as they can be obtained."

The specter of frozen death also hung over both camps, and carried off some wounded Northern boys hospitalized in unheated tents. Many Southerners slept without blankets. The best shelter Billy Yank and Johnny Reb could devise consisted of a hole scraped in the ground, a rude log hut tossed up over it, and all graced, perhaps, with a mud-and-stick chimney. Lee himself wintered in a tent blessed with a stove; he shared his quarters with a hen that earned room and board by laying eggs frequently.

The soldier claimed no monopoly on hardship. With the war in its third year, a bitter harvest was spilling over everywhere. On the little farms of New England and the Midwest, on backcountry plots in Alabama and Arkansas and all the rest, soldiers' wives worked desperately to feed and clothe their young families, and prayed against word of death, which arrived more and more often.

Everybody waited and watched. Towns and cities took back their sons used up in the fray and discarded: hobbling men and empty-sleeved ones. Parts of the South in war's path felt hunger pangs; city folk winced at inflation's pinch and speculators' gouging. In 1860, 10 pounds of bacon had cost $1.25, the Richmond *Dispatch* reported; by 1863, the price skyrocketed to $10. In the same period, 5 pounds of sugar zoomed from 40 cents to $5.75; 3 pounds of *Continued on page 117*

Victims of bombardment recoil in terror from a sputtering Union shell at Vicksburg in June 1863. During a 47-day siege of the Rebels' greatest stronghold on the Mississippi, hunger often forced residents from the shelter of basements and caves. Only a month before, victory in Virginia had raised Confederate hopes, but defeat here and at Gettysburg presaged doom.

Lincoln's Cabinet hears him read his draft of the Emancipation Proclamation; he presented it to them on July 22, 1862, and again two months later. In this painting by Alonzo Chappel, the artist chose as background a view of the Capitol, actually unfinished and not visible from the White House Cabinet Room. The President announced the Proclamation after Union forces turned back Lee's invasion of Maryland at Antietam; it took effect January 1, 1863. The measure focused the war on the issue of slavery and helped induce European powers not to recognize the Confederacy. In the summer of 1863, Federal volunteer Negro troops helped open the 22-month land-and-sea assault on Charleston, South Carolina. Spearheading an unsuccessful attack on Battery Wagner, the 54th Massachusetts Infantry Regiment in hand-to-hand combat suffered 44 percent casualties —including its leader, Col. Robert G. Shaw (with saber, below).

DETAIL FROM PAINTING BY ALONZO CHAPPEL, 1863, BOSTON MUSEUM OF FINE ARTS, KAROLIK COLLECTION (ABOVE); TOM LOVELL

General Burnside's "auspicious moment...to strike a...mortal blow to the rebellion" by flanking Lee and capturing Richmond fades in the abortive Mud March along the Rappahannock. Unrecovered from the month-old calamity at Fredericksburg, morale dropped so low that boos greeted the commander at a troop review and thousands of men deserted. Less known for his leadership than for his luxuriant sidewhiskers, Burnside resigned his command; Lincoln named Maj. Gen. Joseph Hooker to replace him. The ill-starred Burnside (right) reads a newspaper at his headquarters near Falmouth, Virginia. Straw-hatted photographer Mathew Brady gets into the picture, one of about 5,000 scenes he or some 300 other cameramen recorded during the war. The men sat still for half a minute or so for the exposure; plates required immediate development in traveling darkrooms.

WEST POINT MUSEUM, ALEXANDER McCOOK CRAIGHEAD COLLECTION (ABOVE); LIBRARY OF CONGRESS

115

butter from 75 cents to $5.25; 5 pounds of soap from 50 cents to $5.50; 4 pounds of coffee from 50 cents to $20 (and people substituted parched sweet potatoes, parched corn, corn meal, beans, rye, and acorns).

"While my youngest daughter was in the kitchen to-day," noted a Richmond diarist, "a young rat came out of its hole and seemed to beg for something to eat; she held out some bread, which it ate from her hand, and seemed grateful. Several others soon appeared, and were as tame as kittens. Perhaps we shall have to eat them!" (Within a few months, in besieged and starving Vicksburg, mule meat and rancid bacon would hang side by side in the market.)

THE COST OF BOOTS was rising to $50 a pair and more, shoes from $15 to $25. Southern women sewed coverings for their feet from remnants of carpets already cut up for soldiers' blankets. As clothing became unavailable, they improvised further. Varina Howell Davis, handsome and witty wife of President Davis, recalled that hats were plaited from dried and bleached palmetto, with chicken feathers decorating them. "And if one sometimes regretted," Mrs. Davis went on, "that millinery should be a matter of private judgment, still, in their pretty homespun dresses they would have passed favorably in review with any ladies."

Enterprising women also cut old scraps of silk in pieces, carded them, and spun them into fine yarn with which they knitted silk stockings. When this source ran out, the moment of truth arrived. My wife and I know what a friend's great-grandmother, a Virginian, did when she no longer could obtain silk stockings. "She went to bed," our friend told us with a straight face, "and stayed there for eight years."

Bad as it all was, it would grow much worse. Two warring countries existed in the land. Memories of a common glory were buried; the Confederacy would fight to the finish, obdurate as the lady who took to her bed. Though angry disagreements rent each nation, though it now came clear that, without good fortune from some unexpected quarter, the North's bulk eventually must crush the South, the hard truth remained: The house Lincoln spoke of had been divided — and twin dwellings stood. Even without foreign recognition, Southern leaders hoped their country could outlast the North's will to fight. Someone suggested a design for the Confederate seal: a man paddling his own canoe, with the motto "D--n England and France."

Presidents Davis and Lincoln became whipping boys for politicians, plain people, and the press in both nations. Many of their problems sprang from war's oppression. Lee's army had survived the bloodbath at Antietam Creek, yes, and won great victories in Virginia — what did these prove when the Union still menaced Richmond? Many Southerners said it: After 20 months of war, the Confederacy had won only a tenuous stalemate — by suffering deadly attrition.

Beyond this, Jefferson Davis, as dedicated a patriot as ever the Confederacy produced, faced a special nightmare. He had always championed the rights of the states. Now he saw with growing clarity the need for strong central government. He had the crucial task of resolving the continual conflicts between them, and it demanded greater political skill than Davis — proud, austere, and logical — ever possessed.

Blind in one eye from what might have been glaucoma, pained

Lee, astride his beloved Traveller, meets Jackson for the last time after the two comrades-in-arms planned a surprise attack at Chancellorsville, Virginia, for May 2. The classic battle gave Lee a major victory but cost him Jackson, shot by his own men. They mistook Stonewall's party, returning from reconnaissance, for Union cavalry.

intensely by frequent facial neuralgia, nervous and dyspeptic, Davis did his duty as he saw it. He burdened himself with paper work and petty detail that clerks should have handled. He told others just how they were wrong, and his manner did not inspire them to ask if he might be right.

Respecting the South's magnificent effort as I do, I find it a startling incongruity that Davis, so inflexible in office, led the rebellious states in their awesome revolution. Yet Frank E. Vandiver, outstanding historian of the Confederacy, has summed it up: "Jefferson Davis was much like his country." Perhaps one wonders in vain what a different leader, a statesman and politician who could evoke the Constitution's spirit by taking its letter to the fullest, might have accomplished for the Confederate States of America.

Such a man interpreted the Union to itself and the world, though many—possibly most—people were unappreciative until after the assassin's bullet killed Abraham Lincoln.

As 1863 came on, the North had little to show for its war effort but blood and tears. Even in the West, scene of Grant's triumphs, Union gains in Tennessee were checked by resurgent Rebel forces under the curiously inconsistent General Bragg and hard-riding raiders led by the brilliant Nathan Bedford Forrest and the romantic Earl Van Dorn. Though Bragg confounded his officers and men by failing to reap the fruits of victory, he did slow the Union advance. And on December 20, 1862, Van Dorn, by destroying Grant's supply base at Holly Springs, Mississippi, forced the Northern commander to abandon his first campaign against Vicksburg. A few days later, Sherman lost more than 1,700 Federals in a futile assault at Chickasaw Bayou, five miles north of Vicksburg. The South suffered only 200 casualties.

Press, politicians, and ordinary citizens poured venom on the hapless Lincoln. Newspapers scourged him as "the head ghoul at Washington," a "half-witted usurper," and the like; opposition politicians titled him the "original gorilla" and worse; many persons, becoming fed up with the war, blamed the President's choice of generals, harped on his conduct of operations, and ranted at him for speculators' profiteering and mounting inflation.

B Y NOW THRONGS OF NEGROES, liberated as armies warred across the land, found themselves adrift and unwanted. Northern workmen cried out against ex-slaves as competitors. The same soldiers whose blood bought their freedom often reviled them. As thousands of black people streamed into Washington, white opinion hardened against them.

In the face of all this Lincoln issued the Emancipation Proclamation, as he had warned the Confederate States he would. If Jefferson Davis could have offered some measure to end the onus of human bondage, other nations then in conscience could have recognized the Confederacy as an independent republic. She professed to fight for independence, not for slavery; now she must prove it to the world.

It was impossible. Nothing in the Confederate Constitution gave Davis the scope that its counterpart gave Lincoln. The Confederacy left the fate of slavery to the sovereign states—only they could act; they did not. Here lay the South's curse. Protest as she did that she fought only for freedom, the humans she enslaved guaranteed her doom.

Yelling Rebels renew their attack at Chancellorsville a day after Jackson had panicked unsuspecting Yankees. The Federals slowly dropped back to strong defensive lines, but Hooker, disabled and demoralized, ordered retreat, opening the door to Lee's second invasion of the North.

Lincoln believed in state's rights too. He had defined his objection to slavery with golden simplicity—"As I would not be a slave, so I would not be a master"—but he had accepted the fact that the Constitution protected slavery within states that permitted it. Then with the Union at stake he looked beyond the states to the people—to all the people. Perhaps he really had no more power legally to free the slaves than Davis; plenty of critics thought he acted unconstitutionally. He explained his Proclamation as "sincerely believed to be an act of justice, warranted by the Constitution, upon military necessity...."

To the Radicals of Northern politics, the abolitionists, the bitter enemies of slavery, no explanation was needed. They had been demanding this. For, high principles and motives aside, it was Lincoln the pragmatic politician who brought down slavery's house. What a curious document, his Emancipation Proclamation. It let slavery continue in Missouri and Kentucky, Maryland and Delaware; these border states remained in the Union, its Constitution protected them, and Lincoln the realist did not wish to antagonize them. It freed the slaves in rebellious areas—precisely where the Federal authority and Constitution were denied, where he could not enforce it. It was enough. Wherever a Union column appeared slaves fell in behind and followed in sheer faith, and a little more of the Confederacy came apart. Walking, perched on rickety carts, riding ancient mules, they moved along freedom's long road; whatever lay ahead would be better than what they left.

Lincoln welcomed black men into the armed services in the same declaration which called some of them free, and in time nearly 200,000 joined up. And in case conscription became necessary, Congress that spring voted male citizens between 20 and 45 subject to the draft, exempting anyone who paid $300 or found somebody as his substitute.

To crank up the war again, Lincoln accepted Burnside's resignation and turned the Army of the Potomac over to Maj. Gen. Joseph Hooker. Slim, handsome, carrying a fighter's reputation, the 48-year-old West Pointer also bore a reputation for loose talk. In a letter to Hooker, Lincoln gave him a plain warning against intrigue:

"I have heard, in such way as to believe it, of your recently saying that both the Army and the Government needed a Dictator. Of course it was not *for* this, but in spite of it, that I have given you the command. Only those generals who gain successes can set up dictators. What I now ask of you is military success, and I will risk the dictatorship."

"Fighting Joe" Hooker turned out to be a first-rate organizer. By April he rounded the dejected army at Falmouth into shape, ready to prove itself. Hooker felt ready also. "When I get to Richmond . . ." he kept prating, a sensitive subject to the oft-burned President.

Anyone who toils in the Civil War's vineyard marvels at Lincoln's poor fortune with his field commanders. Thus far U. S. Grant alone had pleased him—and Lincoln still needed to see more before giving him full faith. In the East, after two years of war, the failures began with McDowell and extended through McClellan, Pope, McClellan again, and Burnside. Could Hooker at last be the man?

No. When the chips were down, and with far the stronger hand, Hooker folded, all the fight out of him. It happened as April merged with May at a lonely place called Chancellorsville, a road junction with the Chancellor family's home beside it and a thick, grim scrub forest known as the Wilderness just beyond.

He devised a good plan and began it well. His strength came to nearly 134,000 effectives; Lee counted less than half as many. Hooker left one wing of his army to face the Rebels along the old lines at Fredericksburg, while he marched the other wing upriver 30 miles or so and then doubled back down to lodge on Lee's left flank and rear. There he had only to spring the trap. "The rebel army is now the legitimate property of the Army of the Potomac," he bragged, cackling prematurely.

Once in position, however, the Federal commander dallied. By the time he began to move, the aggressive Lee had come up and was probing him. Surprised and confused, Hooker pulled back from relatively high ground and took up defensive positions around Chancellorsville.

Boastful Maj. Gen. Joseph Hooker lost his nerve, 17,000 men, and the President's confidence when Lee outgeneraled him at Chancellorsville. "My God, my God, what will the country say!" Lincoln cried, hearing of the defeat.

His corps commanders objected. "If he thinks he can't hold the top of the hill," growled Maj. Gen. George G. Meade, "how does he expect to hold the bottom of it?"

Military experts call the Battle of Chancellorsville Lee's masterpiece. To produce it, the South's brilliant tactician took daring chances that still excite admiration and wonder. Confronted by a greatly superior enemy, he boldly split his army into three parts. Maj. Gen. Jubal A. Early and 10,000 Confederates already manned the heights at Fredericksburg, watching some 28,000 Union troops under Maj. Gen. John Sedgwick across the Rappahannock. Lee himself, with about 12,000 men, stood against the main Federal force of 73,000 in the vicinity of Chancellorsville. And Stonewall Jackson, in a brash, day-long march across much of the Union front, led 31,700 men into position on Hooker's right flank—outflanking the outflanker.

Hooker got it into his head that Jackson's march meant the Rebels were retreating. Yet he merely ordered the III Corps to advance cautiously and harass the movement. Virtually unhampered, Jackson stole up as afternoon waned on May 2 and crashed out of the Wilderness into the extreme right of Hooker's army while soldiers listened to band music and ate supper. The unsupported Federals struggled vainly and reeled back in chaos, fleeing toward Chancellorsville.

Hoping to exploit his gains, Jackson rode forward in growing darkness to reconnoiter. As he returned, his own troops mistook him for the enemy and shot him three times. The amputation of his left arm followed; Mrs. Jackson came to be with him, bringing their six-month-old daughter.

Stonewall Jackson's haversack and his Napoleon's Maxims of War, *a gift from Maj. Gen. J. E. B. Stuart, rest against the flag that covered Jackson's coffin.*

Cavalryman Jeb Stuart assumed command. Though Jackson's attack had succeeded, Lee's two wings remained apart—a prime opportunity for an alert and combative Hooker to fall on one wing or the other with his superior strength and annihilate it. Instead, as Lee and Stuart renewed the attack at dawn on May 3, he pulled his line in more tightly, and the Southerners battled through to effect a linkup.

Lee learned that Jubal Early's small force had left Fredericksburg and that Sedgwick was advancing toward Chancellorsville. Again Lee split his army, keeping about 36,000 troops to deal with Hooker's much larger array while using the rest to check Sedgwick. The next day Early joined their counterattack and Sedgwick withdrew across the river.

Now Lee turned in strength to attack Hooker, who had neither troubled Stuart, poised before his entrenchments, nor sent aid to Sedgwick. But as the great Southern commander prepared to order the advance, he learned that Hooker had stolen away in the night across the Rappahannock. Soon the Army of the Potomac again settled into the old campsites at Falmouth, opposite Fredericksburg.

Once more Lee took up station across from the Federals, unable to make his dazzling victory a decisive one for his cause. The North could afford far better Chancellorsville's 17,000 casualties than the South its nearly 13,000. The Union army soon would recover and pose a greater menace than ever. And there was something else. Lee had wrestled in prayer for the wounded Stonewall Jackson as he never had for himself. "Give him my affectionate regards," he told one of Jackson's chaplains, "and tell him to make haste and get well, and come back to me as soon as he can. He has lost his left arm, but I have lost my right."

The fighting Presbyterian seemed to be recovering until he contracted pneumonia several days after the battle. The end came rapidly but not before Jackson made his dispositions, completing them as death arrived and summing himself up for all time: "Let us cross over the river," he murmured, "and rest under the shade of the trees."

Lee wept, his sense of loss and personal grief beyond measure. "I know not how to replace him," he sorrowed. When Stonewall Jackson died, the South lost the man who best carried out Lee's dynamic strategy; the Army of Northern Virginia would never be the same. High noon for the Confederate States of America shone over a forlorn country crossroads named Chancellorsville.

Richmond mourned Jackson but rejoiced in the victory. For the fourth time General Lee had managed to keep the Union at bay. Still, perceptive men worried; grievous problems loomed in the West.

Both sides shared a shortcoming in Civil War operations: One hand often did not know what the other was doing. The lack of coordination between what the Union sought to accomplish in the eastern, western, and trans-Mississippi theaters continued until 1864. It was worse in the Confederacy. And state's rights blurred overall strategy; the South really fought not one war but several.

Part of her problems centered in Tennessee. There, as 1863 began, Davis's friend General Bragg—mistrusted by his men for backing away from his promising 1862 campaign in Kentucky—won a brief success at Stone's River over Maj. Gen. William S. Rosecrans. But Bragg failed to crush the Union force or drive it from the field. Again he pulled back in retreat, and by summer slow-moving Rosecrans began pushing him southeast toward Chattanooga.

Worse trouble by far was developing in Mississippi. Bulldog-like Ulysses S. Grant was setting his Army of the Tennessee at Vicksburg's throat, as he had long aimed to do. Why this sultry little Mississippi River port of 4,600 souls? Its prewar traffic with the northwest had brought prosperity, and it had voted against the hotheads of secession.

Since August 1862, the Union Navy had controlled the Mississippi as far downstream as Vicksburg, and from New Orleans upstream to Port Hudson, Louisiana. The Confederacy commanded the 250 river miles between these two strongholds, and fought to save communications with her states beyond the west bank—Texas, Arkansas, and most of Louisiana. Lincoln was determined to re-open the river, and Port Hudson would pose no special difficulties once Vicksburg fell.

But Vicksburg's snarling batteries, which dominated a three-mile sweep of the river from 200-foot-high bluffs above the eastern shore, denied the continent's great water highway to the Nation. The Navy already had tried to reduce the city by bombardment, and concluded that it would take an army to conquer her.

Jane and the children and I flew to Mississippi to see what Grant had to do. Standing above the city on those same bluffs in Vicksburg National Military Park, it seemed to me that Grant's perseverance—and Lincoln's patience—approached the superhuman. Five times the stubborn general reached out to capture the city, and failed, while the

LITHOGRAPH, 1863, U.S. NAVAL ACADEMY MUSEUM (TOP); LIBRARY OF CONGRESS; MAP BY RICHARD SCHLECHT

The War in the West: Rear Adm. David D. Porter (left) runs his fleet downstream past booming guns on the 200-foot bluffs of Vicksburg. With the transports he brought, the Union army crossed the Mississippi to Bruinsburg, and Grant struck inland. Heading northeast, he took Jackson, shunting aside Rebel reinforcements, then turned west to attack Vicksburg from the rear.

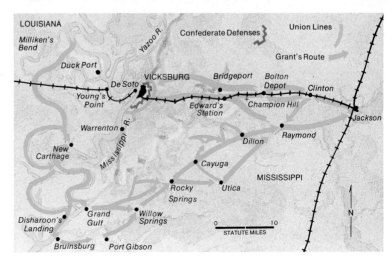

123

Minié balls from Vicksburg's defenders tear into Federal troops struggling past sharpened stakes and up scaling ladders. Unable to take the city by assault, Grant's army laid siege. On July 4, a day

after Lee's defeat at Gettysburg, Vicksburg surrendered. Its fall split the South, opening the whole
Mississippi to Union traffic. "The Father of Waters," Lincoln wrote, "again goes unvexed to the sea."

Chief Executive staved off increasing pressure to fire him. Grant succeeded on the sixth attempt, after seven months of herculean effort.

With an 11-year-old's straightforward curiosity, Robbie asked what caused all the difficulty. Mostly geography, I replied. Like people and weather, geography plays a major role in war.

To the north spread the Delta, a soggy floodplain laced with bayous and bogs, checkered in those days with dense forests and choked with brush, almost impenetrable except by boat. Along Vicksburg's western edge flowed the Mississippi. On the south, the bluffs continued along the east bank, while swampy lowlands militated against a march down the Louisiana side. Grant must try to capture Vicksburg from the east. But how to get there?

On the river's Louisiana bank, Grant first set his men to digging a mile-long canal across DeSoto Peninsula, just below the city; Lincoln hoped this would divert the Mississippi through it. A sudden rise in the river flooded them out. He sent expedition after expedition through bayou country, all of which bogged down for one reason or another.

Undismayed, the Union general marched his army down the river's west side to draw up at Hard Times plantation. Across the wide waters and four miles east rose the ghost of Grand Gulf, 24 miles below Vicksburg. Once the town was a booming cotton port, but the shifting Mississippi had gnawed away most of it by 1860. On bluffs above the ravaged town waited strongly entrenched Rebel infantry and artillery.

From Hard Times, Grant intended to ferry troops to Grand Gulf and storm the fortifications. Rear Adm. David D. Porter had gunboats and transports anchored north of Vicksburg; to carry the army across the river, they first must run the city's fiery gantlet.

About midnight April 16—as Confederate officers and their crinolined beauties danced at a gay military ball—Porter sent part of his little fleet downstream. The armada consisted of seven armored vessels, a ram, and three transports; the ships sailed 50 feet apart, with the transports protected on their port sides by logs and bales of cotton and hay.

Confederate pickets spotted the procession and gave the alarm. Eerie light leaped from flaming tar barrels and blazing buildings, illuminating the dark, gliding silhouettes for Rebel cannoneers. "Their heavy shot walked right through us," said Porter, in a "magnificent, but terrible" spectacle which lasted two and a half hours. "Every fort and hilltop vomited forth shot and shell." Miraculously, only one ship was sunk. A few nights later more transports and supply barges slipped past.

It proved different when the doughty admiral tried to silence Grand Gulf's batteries for Grant's amphibious assault. The seven gunboats with 80-odd cannon hammered at the Rebel positions, which mounted much less ordnance. Shells screamed for more than five hours before the Navy, heavily damaged, ceased fire and withdrew. "Grand Gulf," declared a rueful Porter, "is the strongest place on the Mississippi."

That night the fleet eased south, steaming eight miles to Disharoon's Plantation on the Louisiana side while the army marched there. Next morning, April 30, the Navy ferried more than 22,000 men across the river and landed them unopposed at the village of Bruinsburg. I think Grant must have been shaking his head. "When this was effected," he admitted, "I felt a degree of relief scarcely ever equalled since.... I was

Corinthian columns alone remain of Windsor, once called Mississippi's handsomest house. When Grant first saw the plantation home near Port Gibson, scene of his first victory on the sweep to Vicksburg, he thought it a Confederate lookout post. Undamaged by Union guns, it served as a hospital after the fight. The mansion stood until it burned in 1890.

now in the enemy's country, with a vast river and the stronghold of Vicksburg between me and my base of supplies. But I was on dry ground on the same side of the river with the enemy." The enemy gathered strength to oppose him. Gen. Joe Johnston came from Tennessee to take command and raise a force to join the garrison from Vicksburg.

But in 20 days the Federals marched about 180 miles and defeated the two Rebel armies separately in vicious fights at Port Gibson, Raymond, Jackson, Champion Hill, and on the Big Black River. Then they came up in back of Vicksburg, tried to storm its defenses, suffered brutal repulses, and laid siege. Eventually Grant's strength totaled 76,000 men, but it took 47 days to win this stronghold. Guarded by steep slopes on the east, Vicksburg proved a natural fortress.

MY FAMILY AND I followed Grant's path, occasionally turning up traces of the old rancor. The North laid heavy hand here during the war and afterward, and remembrance passes from father to son. Much oftener, we applauded the South's manifest pride of heritage and the honor it pays those who struggled so valiantly a century ago.

An outstanding exemplar of this, a genial, soft-spoken resident of Port Gibson named William D. Lum, escorted us to Grand Gulf. He captivated Robbie, Meredith, and Julia as he set the old scene: steamboats rounding the bend with black smoke pouring from twin stacks, slaves rousting cotton bales on the landing, locomotive chuffing at the depot, stores and houses all about us. Jane and I, though, had difficulty visualizing this. We could see only a handful of silvered shacks sagging where 76 city blocks once spread. Even the fickle river had remade its bed out of sight to the west; somewhere out there in the dried-up old channel—Bill Lum knew where—reposed the skeleton of the sunken Union gunboat *Rattler*. Nothing disturbed the solitude except redbirds flashing among the trees and a deer bounding through the canebrake.

Yet Grand Gulf offers a strong presence. The memory of those who fought there lives on, commemorated by Grand Gulf Military Monument. Mr. Lum and his fellow park commissioners have stripped away time's increment. Trenches and gun emplacements stand out clearly; parapet and site of the hot shot furnace are still visible. Rifle pits rim a

Sun-gilded swamp north of Vicksburg silhouettes a fisherman. Before striking at Bruinsburg, Grant sent four unsuccessful expeditions through flooded country like this, trying to find a route from the Mississippi up to the high ground where Vicksburg lay. The maneuvers kept his army's morale high, satisfied Northern demands for action, and kept the enemy guessing.

Gettysburg: Federals behind rocks and breastworks at the base of Culp's Hill fire into Rebels charging down a ridge late on the morning of July 3. In this final assault, the third in seven hours, attackers who reached the defenses died or surrendered. All along the Union line, Federal soldiers commanded by nervous, quick-tempered Maj. Gen. George G. Meade (right) held against repeated Rebel attempts to storm their positions. Only three days before the battle began, Meade had learned with astonishment that Lincoln ordered him to lead the Army of the Potomac.

P. F. ROTHERMEL, C. 1868, PENNSYLVANIA HISTORICAL AND MUSEUM COMMISSION, HARRISBURG (ABOVE); THOMAS HICKS, 1876, MILITARY ORDER OF THE LOYAL LEGION, PHILADELPHIA

cemetery presided over by venerable, moss-hung cedars; crumbling headstones tell of yellow fever and cholera, steamboat explosions and tornadoes, of men who never made it to the gold rush in California, of death by murder and by peaceful old age.

The park's museum tells other tales. In one corner rests a Confederate limber and caisson, recovered only recently from the Big Black River. Robbie and I could picture what happened: Rebel engineers hastily throwing a pontoon bridge across the Big Black; exhausted soldiers stumbling across it, retreating from Champion Hill toward Vicksburg before the relentless Grant. Suddenly an ammunition-heavy limber and caisson, drawn by six straining mules, crashes through the planks. A century and more later, one of the wheels emerges and men painstakingly exhume the rare find. The river also yields up the ammunition chest and 139 three-inch shells.

Mr. Lum pointed out a faded maroon sash framed on a museum wall.

Richard Schlecht

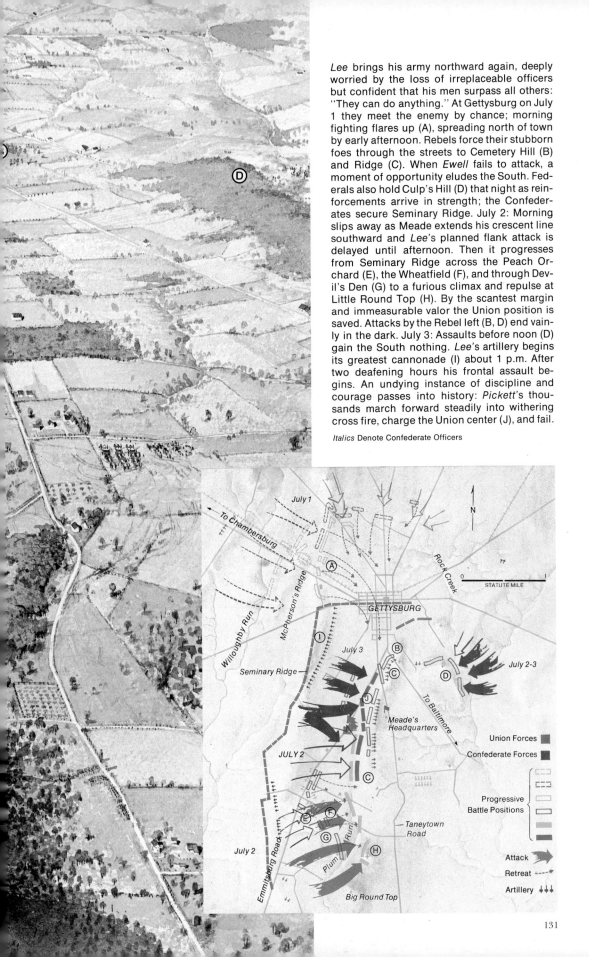

Lee brings his army northward again, deeply worried by the loss of irreplaceable officers but confident that his men surpass all others: "They can do anything." At Gettysburg on July 1 they meet the enemy by chance; morning fighting flares up (A), spreading north of town by early afternoon. Rebels force their stubborn foes through the streets to Cemetery Hill (B) and Ridge (C). When *Ewell* fails to attack, a moment of opportunity eludes the South. Federals also hold Culp's Hill (D) that night as reinforcements arrive in strength; the Confederates secure Seminary Ridge. July 2: Morning slips away as Meade extends his crescent line southward and *Lee*'s planned flank attack is delayed until afternoon. Then it progresses from Seminary Ridge across the Peach Orchard (E), the Wheatfield (F), and through Devil's Den (G) to a furious climax and repulse at Little Round Top (H). By the scantest margin and immeasurable valor the Union position is saved. Attacks by the Rebel left (B, D) end vainly in the dark. July 3: Assaults before noon (D) gain the South nothing. *Lee*'s artillery begins its greatest cannonade (I) about 1 p.m. After two deafening hours his frontal assault begins. An undying instance of discipline and courage passes into history: *Pickett*'s thousands march forward steadily into withering cross fire, charge the Union center (J), and fail.

Italics Denote Confederate Officers

131

He said, "My great-grandfather, Maj. Robert Cochran McCay, was killed at the Battle of Harrisburg, Mississippi, in 1864. His body servant, Squire Jackson, walked by night and slept in woods by day for weeks to bring word home, carrying Major McCay's sash, sword, and watch. Yes, those are bloodstains. I remember Squire Jackson, though I was only three or four when he died. The whole family went to his funeral."

Our host also told us a story about U. S. Grant: Soon after the Union commander crossed the river, he stayed briefly at a house not far from us. Learning that the son of the house, a Confederate soldier, lay sick there, he sent his surgeon to treat him. When Grant moved on, the doctor left medicine and told the boy's mother how to care for him.

Grant's long blue columns followed several country roads over his angular route to Vicksburg and military immortality. One column tramped past the hamlet of Rocky Springs, today a wide spot in the road just off the Natchez Trace with only the brick church still standing. A way of life died as the Union men came through, and I know of no better example than what befell a nearby plantation, Vernalia.

Bill Lum drove us there. In 1851, he told us, the widow Sinai Lum built the commodious house, a frame Southern-planter-type dwelling. One of her four children, Mary Elizabeth, married the ill-fated Major McCay; this was his home until he left, never to return.

Constructed of cypress and oak, sitting on rocks hand-shaped there, Vernalia crowned a breeze-swept knoll shaded by colossal trees. Not a grand mansion, it typified the homes of many working planters. Across the 60-foot front ran a spacious gallery supported by sturdy posts of cypress. A wide center hall opened to large, high-ceilinged rooms with white plastered walls and green blinds; the second floor contained bedrooms and a storage area. People called it the coolest house in Mississippi on a summer afternoon.

Beyond rested the cookhouse and slave quarters, for the plantation's acres swelled across the Big Black's valleys and hills and its slaves grew cotton and corn under an overseer's eye. Seamstresses made clothes in one building here; in another, an old woman cared for the babies, and their mothers came in from the fields every three hours to nurse them. By the flower garden stood a small schoolhouse; the Lum children always had a tutor or governess from the North.

Vernalia prospered. Life was good. The plantation produced most of its own food, and there was plenty for all. Children romped on the wide lawn while their Sunday-calling parents chatted on the veranda. Bookcases were filled with popular and classic works. Over all, religion imposed gentle authority.

Early in May 1863, Union troops arrived and pitched tents in the yard. Despite express orders, they dug up the family's buried silver, appropriated livestock and chickens, and raided the house. Freedom came to the slaves. When the Federals departed, the world had turned over.

The family managed to hang on down the years, and descendants still live at Vernalia. Time, I could see, has continued its cruelties. The once-proud plantation house creaks beneath its ancient oaks, elms, and cedars, a monument to adversity, a weary and gray shell wearing its years like a shroud. Bill Lum saddens to see it.

The fortunes of war fell even more harshly elsewhere as Grant

As his father watches, Robbie Jordan clambers among the boulders in Devil's Den at Gettysburg. Rebels, pushing hard toward Little Round Top on the afternoon of July 2, dislodged Union troops from these jumbled rocks and installed their own men.

advanced. At Jackson, Gen. Joe Johnston retreated before Sherman and James B. McPherson. Sherman ordered public property burned; people stared at naked smokestacks and came to call it "Chimneyville."

At Vicksburg, Grant embraced the fortifications in an ever-tightening clasp that began at the river and curled along the crest of a ridge to the lowlands south of the city. The Union Navy's bombardment over 14 months flung more than 22,000 shells; by one estimate, Grant tossed in 2,800 every 24 hours for more than a month and a half.

The city turned into rubble. People lived in cellars and caves, dipped water from mud holes, slowly starved, and prayed.

Lt. Gen. John C. Pemberton, a native of Philadelphia whose Southern sympathies began with his Virginia-born wife, commanded Vicksburg's defenses. A mediocre general, he had gotten conflicting instructions from Jefferson Davis and Joe Johnston to add to his woes at a time when he was confronted with U. S. Grant. On the Fourth of July, his situation hopeless, he marched his men out in front of their works, stacked arms and colors, and surrendered.

The Union had taken more than 10,000 casualties since its men set foot on the shore at Bruinsburg. The Confederacy had lost 9,000. Pemberton handed over nearly 30,000 more, with quantities of irreplaceable guns and ammunition. Port Hudson surrendered five days later. Abraham Lincoln summed it up in a simple, poetic sentence. "The Father of Waters," he wrote, "again goes unvexed to the sea."

Vicksburg made its own comment. In a house pocked by shot and shell, the strange quiet closed in on a man and he turned to his wife and spoke: "It seems to me I can hear the silence, and feel it, too. It wraps me like a soft garment; how else can I express this peace?" And Vicksburg would remember. Not until 1945 could she bring herself to observe Independence Day.

Control of the Mississippi cleaved the Confederacy from north to south, severing the lifeline from Rebel states to the west. Now Union armies could sling their knapsacks for new fields to the east — fields where victories would inevitably split the South into smaller pieces. And all the while Hooker's fine Army of the Potomac, outgeneraled but

On Little Round Top, the author recalls for his family the savage fighting there. Daughter Julia, age 5, leans against 11-year-old Robbie. Meredith, 7, sits between the author and his wife Jane. Federal troops wrestled half a dozen 10-pounder Parrotts up the rocky slopes during Longstreet's assault that almost took the hill, key to the Union line.

NATIONAL GEOGRAPHIC PHOTOGRAPHER JOSEPH J. SCHERSCHEL

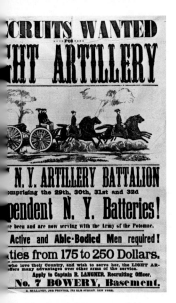

always valiant, threatened Richmond from its encampment at Falmouth.

The fatal outline had emerged clearly to Confederate leaders before Vicksburg fell, of course. Something had to be done and early in June Robert E. Lee did it, setting off to invade the North once more. No longer able to feed and clothe his soldiers in ravaged Virginia, he was carrying the war to a land of plenty. He still believed that victory on foreign soil might bring peace closer. Perhaps—a last faint gleam of hope—European recognition would finally be won.

A tremendous gamble, this, but Lee specialized in long odds. At Falmouth, with most of the Rebel host departed, Hooker proposed to strike for Richmond. Lincoln declined: "I think *Lee's* Army, and not *Richmond*, is your true objective point," he said.

So the walking war resumed in the East. Lee's 75,000 gaunt Rebels, strung out on an arc of 50 miles, moved northwest from Fredericksburg screened by Jeb Stuart's cavalry. On June 9, at Brandy Station, Federal horsemen under Maj. Gen. Alfred Pleasonton attacked Stuart. They collided in furious charge and countercharge, galloping into one another for hours for close work with sabers and revolvers. The contest ended with Stuart holding the field, but the Union horsemen with their long-standing inferiority complex finally came into their own that day—in the last great cavalry battle of classic style.

The Confederacy's gray columns trooped on, through gaps in the Blue Ridge and northeast through Stonewall Jackson's old hunting grounds, the Shenandoah Valley. Hooker began the chase and on June 14, Lincoln, pre-eminent prodder of generals, sent another barb: "If the head of Lee's army is at Martinsburg and the tail of it . . . between Fredericksburg and Chancellorsville, the animal must be very slim somewhere. Could you not break him?"

Up the Shenandoah Valley, across the Potomac into Maryland, through the Cumberland Valley and into Pennsylvania—unbroken—strode the ragged host, striking fear into the North. As June waned, crusty Maj. Gen. Jubal Early extracted $28,000 from the city of York; his one-legged, bald superior, Lt. Gen. Richard S. Ewell, captured Chambersburg and sent a division toward Harrisburg, Pennsylvania's capital. Washington grew tense; Philadelphia trembled.

One thing deeply troubled Lee. He could find out nothing about the enemy. Where was Hooker? Lee's eyes and ears—Jeb Stuart's cavalry—had failed him. With discretionary orders, the cavalier Stuart was off with most of the cavalry, conducting his own invasion. The Yankees marched north between him and Lee, and Stuart was forced into detours and delays. Not until July 2 could he report to his commander.

On June 28, while Lee camped near Chambersburg, two things happened that irrevocably altered the South's fortunes and those of a peaceful town named Gettysburg. Lee learned, from a spy, that

Billboards and posters announce cash bonuses to attract volunteers; young men had become disenchanted with a prolonged war. Southern states filled army quotas for one year, Northern states for two. When Union recruiting dwindled, Congress passed a conscription act. Anti-draft mobs in New York killed about a dozen people, mostly Negroes, and destroyed property, including a Negro orphanage (far left). Troops quelling the riot killed or wounded more than 1,000.

Hooker's army had crossed the Potomac and threatened his rear elements. And meanwhile Lincoln, gladly accepting Hooker's resignation, turned the command over to able, irascible George G. Meade.

Lee acted immediately to concentrate his dispersed forces, ordering them to assemble eight miles northwest of Gettysburg, at Cashtown.

On June 30, as units of both armies touched lightly at Gettysburg, Meade sent word to his troops: ". . . immense issues involved . . . enemy on our soil . . . Homes, firesides, and domestic altars are involved." And then the clincher: "Corps and other commanders are authorized to order the instant death of any soldier who fails in his duty at this hour."

The holocaust struck July 1, demons in gray swirling in from the west and north to fight their way through the little town. Dogged men in blue drew back to Cemetery Hill, Cemetery Ridge, and Culp's Hill.

The Federals had not yet arrived in full strength as July 2 dawned, and Lee intended General Longstreet to smash early into Meade's left flank while Ewell engaged the right. Neither attack began until late afternoon and by then the bluecoats thronged Cemetery Ridge. The Rebels attacked valiantly; it was close, but the North held. New names were written in blood: the Peach Orchard, the Wheat Field, Devil's Den, Little Round Top.

That night, Meade studied the situation and anticipated an attack at the center of his line on Cemetery Ridge the next day. Lee obliged.

Rebel banner waves over Sumter af

I HAVE PAUSED at that center many times, beside the target clump of trees on Cemetery Ridge near which the men of Pickett's Charge won death and defeat and immortality. The land stays the same: an open field sloping gently down, gently up, to tree-lined Seminary Ridge a mile west. I look across that mile and the chilling presence of the terrible thing that happened here, always hovering, lays hold. Men stream from the ridge's dark woods and form into line, red banners on high, a phantom army of the South's finest. George Pickett gallops to front-center; it is time. General Armistead's white head bobs this way and that, checking his brigade; he sticks his hat on his sword, turns his horse toward the clump of trees: "Forward, guide center! March!"

Off they go, some 13,000 soldiers building a legend for the ages, striding toward death as if on parade. Union canister begins discriminating among them, thinning out the forest of gleaming bayonets. The Confederacy closes ranks and presses on. Up the slope now; into the charge at doubletime. Colors fall amidst smoke and roar. Flaming Federal rifles behind a stone wall shred the attackers. Only a few Rebels live to breach the line, too few; Armistead goes down among them, sword in hand. The grand assault fails. Back go the survivors; less than half of those who stepped off so proudly, 20 minutes earlier, return to Seminary Ridge. Lee speaks to the grieving Pickett: "Come, General Pickett, this has been my fight and upon my shoulders rests the blame."

Late next day, the Fourth of July, as Grant's troops strode triumphantly into Vicksburg, Lee's ambulance train began creaking toward Virginia—a 17-mile-long procession of springless wagons jolting over rutted roads in a driving rain. Wounded and dying men cried out in agony for death's release.

Before long the Army of Northern Virginia was retreating toward

English artist Frank Vizetelly (left), in Charleston during the Union siege by sea, sketched defenders (right) sandbagging a casemate at Fort Sumter. Battered by Federal shore units and ironclads, its brick top tier collapsed around remaining walls, combining with reinforcing dirt and cotton bales to form an even stronger rampart. Despite some 46,000 projectiles, the Rebels held the fortification until they evacuated Charleston.

22 months of Union shelling. Maj. Gen. Robert Anderson saw the colors he struck in 1861 raised there four years later.

In the western theater, as the year wears on, Gen. *Braxton Bragg,* CSA, gives ground in Tennessee before Maj. Gen. William S. Rosecrans, who pries him out of Chattanooga into mountainous country of northwest Georgia. There Chickamauga Creek, winding through dark woodland, separates the armies until the morning of September 19. Then Confederates engage the enemy at Reed's Bridge (A) and advance, probing, as other columns cross the stream (B) and meet to form in line of battle (C). As the fighting spreads and losses climb, the Federals slowly fall back until their left curves around the Kelly Farm (D) and their right extends to the Widow Glenn's (E), the line they hold that night. Near midnight *Longstreet* arrives with men of his corps; *Bragg* reorganizes his command—now *Polk* will take the right wing, *Longstreet* the left. Next day the spearhead of *Longstreet*'s attack strikes a gap in the line (F); he drives through and routs the Union right. Rose-

Italics Denote Confederate Officers

crans flees as the Southerners wheel to take the hills of Horseshoe Ridge (G). On Snodgrass Hill George H. Thomas—the only superior officer left on the field—organizes a last stand. He fights tenaciously, but with decreasing effect, till Granger brings up two brigades (H). As the day wanes, so does the battle; the broken Federals quit the field, escaping northwest to Chattanooga. The South gains the brief elation of a hollow victory, Thomas his enduring fame as "Rock of Chickamauga."

Union Forces

Lines, First day

Lines, A.M., Second day

Lines, P.M., Second day

Retreat ----▶

Confederate Forces

Attack, First day

Attack, Second day

0   2
STATUTE MILES

home. Its reported losses alone came to 20,451, the Union's to 23,045.

Meade, badly mauled and aware that Lee remained dangerous, did not pursue in force for days. When he finally did, it was too late; the foe was safely across the Potomac. Abraham Lincoln was anguished. He wrote reproachfully to Meade, stressing "the magnitude of the misfortune involved in Lee's escape," for "to have closed upon him would . . . have ended the war. . . . Your golden opportunity is gone. . . ."

Having penned this bitter letter, the President then changed his mind. "Never sent, or signed," he scrawled on the envelope. After all, Meade had done a great deal for his country.

I know of no field of honor that tells its story better than Gettysburg National Military Park. Yet nothing so truly reveals the meaning of Gettysburg and the Civil War as a few words Lincoln spoke here on November 19, 1863. He came up from Washington by train to the little Pennsylvania town that would never be the same, rode a horse out to the new burial ground where Union battle dead would continue to be interred for months, and looked out across his divided land with a prophet's vision. Speaking, he lifted his people up and showed them whence they came and whither tended. He pointed to their purpose, told them to get on with their great task, and dedicated them to it. When he finished, he thought his Gettysburg Address a failure. But men still cling to his words, and shall, holding them as a beacon to steer by, seeing in them the profound and soaring meaning of the United States of America.

The immediate task, of course, was to resolve the war. Back again on Virginia soil, Union and Confederacy glowered at each other, sparred a bit, and rested like weary prizefighters between rounds. Nothing conclusive would happen in the East for the rest of the year.

Out in the West, war's hell began breaking loose again. Rebel raider John Hunt Morgan swept through Kentucky, southeastern Indiana, and into Ohio, plundering the countryside until his capture late in July. A month later about 60,000 Federals led by General Rosecrans began to outflank Chattanooga, gateway to Georgia and the Deep South and a vital rail center with links to the rest of the Confederacy. The defenders, 47,000 tough Rebels under Braxton Bragg, pulled back to northwest Georgia to await reinforcements.

Moving deliberately, Rosecrans left Chattanooga behind and set off in quest of Bragg. A few miles southeast, where dark Chickamauga Creek flows, the two armies fought desperately on September 19 and 20, and the Union took a severe whipping. Bragg's main reinforcements —Longstreet's corps from the Army of Northern Virginia—arrived by train in time to smash through a hole in the Union line and cut it in half. Routed, Rosecrans and his men fled back to Chattanooga. A superb last-stand action by Maj. Gen. George H. Thomas prevented complete chaos; Thomas became known as the "Rock of Chickamauga," and Rosecrans presently lost his job to him.

Before or since, the world has never witnessed anything quite like Longstreet's rail movement from Virginia. The South's railroads amounted to a congeries of rickety lines on the point of collapse, with new rails and rolling stock unavailable. Sometimes they lacked bridges, often they failed to connect, they had different gauges, and generally they ran only short distances. A logistician's nightmare, they contributed

Trees blaze with autumn color along Chickamauga Creek near Lee and Gordon's Mills, 12 miles south of Chattanooga. Rebels under Braxton Bragg and Federals under William S. Rosecrans massed along opposite sides of the densely wooded stream in September 1863. Bragg's men began crossing to attack the Federal troops late on the 18th; in the two-day battle that followed nearly one of every three soldiers engaged became a casualty.

His men called Maj. Gen. George H. Thomas "Pap"; the Union knew him as "the Rock of Chickamauga." Left alone on the field after Rebels exploited a gap and routed the Federal right, Thomas and his troops resisted and held until ordered to withdraw.

Autumn a century after Chickamauga: Fallen leaves lie in the muzzle of a 12-pounder Napoleon, the standard Civil War fieldpiece, on Snodgrass Hill where General Thomas and his men made their valiant stand.

greatly to the South's ultimate breakdown. In this instance, to top it off, Longstreet's corps could not take the most direct route, via Knoxville; General Burnside, of Fredericksburg repute, held part of the line by virtue of his operations in east Tennessee.

Call it a minor miracle, then. Around 15,000 battle-hardened veterans piled aboard every kind of railroad car that could roll and used 16 different lines to travel between 800 and 900 miles through Virginia, North and South Carolina, and Georgia. Mary Boykin Chesnut, the Civil War's most charming and perspicacious diarist, glimpsed a passing troop train: ". . . What seemed miles of platform cars, and soldiers rolled in their blankets lying in rows with their heads all covered, fast asleep. In their grey blankets . . . they looked like swathed mummies." She mourned for those who were about to die in their youth.

She had reason. At Chickamauga, Bragg lost about 16,000 men killed, wounded, or missing; Rosecrans, 16,000. And again Bragg did not reap the fruits of victory. By the time he had caught up with the shattered Federals, they had dug in at Chattanooga.

Bragg laid siege. His hungry and badly used soldiers were deserting, and a group of his generals, disgusted and fearing disaster, petitioned the government to fire him. Davis came out; heads rolled, but not Bragg's. He tightened the siege, controlling almost all traffic into the city from positions on commanding heights and in valleys south and west. By mid-October, when Northern reinforcements began arriving and Grant took command, Union soldiers were close to starvation.

Fifteen thousand of those reinforcements came from the Army of the Potomac in another great rail transfer. Headed by Fighting Joe Hooker, the general who was mesmerized at Chancellorsville, they entrained in Virginia and clattered 1,192 miles in just six days via Washington, Baltimore, Columbus, Indianapolis, Louisville, and Nashville, finally reaching the end of their ride at Bridgeport, Alabama. Seventeen thousand additional men under William T. Sherman traveled a roundabout 675 miles from the Vicksburg area by boat, train, and on foot to reach Chattanooga on November 23.

The pugnacious Grant, every bit as businesslike as Robert E. Lee, wasted no time. In the next two days he attacked Confederate positions on the hills overlooking Chattanooga. People in the North heard pleasant-sounding names like Orchard Knob, Lookout Mountain, and Missionary Ridge and found them especially sweet, tasting of victory.

Braxton Bragg retreated into Georgia, and resigned; Joe Johnston succeeded him. One man still believed in Bragg, and gave him work; he became military adviser to President Davis. As the days of 1863 ticked away, the Union held the Confederacy at bay in Virginia, controlled the Mississippi Valley, and stood at the gate to the Deep South. The Confederacy's fortunes were dying.

Back at Orchard Knob, the "Rock of Chickamauga" put men to preparing a military cemetery. The officer who would bury the Union dead asked Thomas if he should inter the slain soldiers by states; after all, they served in Ohio regiments, and Wisconsin regiments, and Michigan, and Indiana, and . . .

"No," said the Virginia-born general. "No, mix 'em up, mix 'em up. I'm tired of state's rights."

Some 60,000 Union soldiers under Rosecrans occupy abandoned Rebel camps near Tullahoma, Tennessee. On August 16 the Federal troops moved out and crossed the Tennessee River at Lookout Mountain (background), forced Chattanooga's evacuation, then withdrew to the city September 22

LITHOGRAPH, C. 1863, AFTER A. E. MATHEWS, A. S. K. BROWN MILITARY COLLECTION, BROWN UNIVERSITY

after their defeat at Chickamauga. Confederates under Bragg laid siege. Lincoln sent troops by train from Mississippi and Virginia, and put Grant in charge. He opened a line for provisions, smashed Bragg's army on November 25, and gave Sherman a supply base for his Atlanta campaign. 143

Grant (left) visits the spot near the crest of Lookout Mountain where Union soldiers had waved a victory flag a few days before. On a rocky shelf halfway up the
peak, Hooker's men on November 24 swept back defenders until heavy fog halted
the action. Observers below romanticized the obscured fight into the "Battle Above
the Clouds." During the night the Confederate troops withdrew from their
defensive positions atop the mountain, now called Point Park (right). President
Lincoln soon named Grant commander of all Union land forces; promoted to
Lieutenant General, he personally directed the campaign to destroy Lee's army.

1864:
DESIGN FOR DESOLATION

CHAPTER FIVE

WORKMEN TOILED away on the growing United States Capitol as 1864 arrived, creating the monumental edifice we see today, while Washington society frolicked. Each fairly exemplified the state of the Union. Newly set in place, the bronze goddess of Freedom crowned the great tiered dome of the Capitol. To Lincoln, construction was "a sign we intend the Union shall go on." Partying at fashionable balls and gay soirées, the high-placed and well-born had no doubt of it. Wine and music, tinkling laughter, clinking glasses and cannonading corks — the North was winning the war, and the North was prospering. Dancing the polka, one had to strain to hear what Lincoln heard plainly: bereaved families at their tears, war-weary citizens urging peace at the price of disunion.

Another sparkling social season rang out in Richmond, but this one wore a down-at-the-heels look, the gentility making light of its shabbiness and chattering with anxiety's forced gaiety. President and Mrs. Davis attended jolly theatricals; everybody lionized visiting heroes. Raider John Hunt Morgan, recently escaped from prison in Ohio, heard the city's acclaim; he would be dead within the year. Romantic Jeb Stuart, swashbuckler in cavalry jacket and high boots, caught the girls' fancy; soon he too would die. John Bell Hood, "the gallant Hood," hobbled in on crutches for his glass of mead, epitome of the desecrated South with left arm crippled at Gettysburg and right leg lost at Chickamauga; soon he would fight again in Georgia and Tennessee and thousands of soldiers would fall uselessly because of his poor judgment.

The Confederacy could have quit right then and saved many lives, if not its cause. Dread portents rose everywhere. Much of Virginia, "battleground and sepulchre of armies," lay torn and bleeding, a shell. Union hosts, strengthened and reorganized, stood poised for a concerted thrust into the Deep South's vitals, and the Army of the Potomac would hurl itself against the gaunt Army of Northern Virginia as soon as spring's sun dried winter's mud.

Empty expression of a Rebel picket reflects the war-weariness of a nation after three years of bloody conflict. Artist Conrad Wise Chapman, who served the Confederacy as a private, painted the picket as a self-portrait, perhaps to record his own disillusionment with the war.

Southerners struggled to keep clothed and fed, caught between their ravenous armies and the ever-tightening blockade. The cost of living escalated almost daily, and the Confederate dollar dwindled; by early 1864 it was worth a Yankee nickel. A well-to-do lady gave $280 for 24 yards of flannel to make into shirts for Johnny Reb. Boots cost $200, a man's "genteel suit," $700. In Richmond, a barrel of flour sold for $150 at New Year's, $200 two weeks later, $300 by March 12. Peace must be had on any terms, or starvation, declared a Raleigh, North Carolina, newspaper. It spoke for many — but not most.

For the South would fight on, unconvinced. Ideas popped up for rescuing the collapsing cause. Make the Confederacy a dictatorship with

"Inhuman, fiendish butchery," Harper's Weekly *called the "massacre" at Fort Pillow, a Union garrison in Tennessee overrun on April 12, 1864. Northern accounts charged that inflamed Rebels, shouting "No quarter!" killed many Negro troops after they had surrendered. The Southerners maintained that the Federals died in fighting before the surrender. In Congress, the Committee on the Conduct of the War accused the South of atrocities, and the North's propaganda machine fueled the passions of the populace. Noble causes had degenerated into "butchery" and nightmarish struggles against personal discomforts like the clinging mud (right) hindering Union artillerymen in "Bringing Up the Guns."*

HARPER'S WEEKLY, 1864, TINTED BY P. HALL BAGLIE (ABOVE); ENGRAVING AFTER GILBERT GAUL, 1889, A. S. K. BROWN MILITARY COLLECTION, BROWN UNIVERSITY

ALBERT BIERSTADT, 1862, THE CENTURY ASSOCIATION, NEW YORK CITY

Robert E. Lee at the head, urged the Lynchburg *Virginian*. Marse Robert would have no part of this, of course. The invaders camped on his country's soil; he must confront them. If he could contain the Federals at least for a few months, and General Johnston in Georgia could handle the Northern horde facing him, Lincoln might fail of re-election in the fall—and a peace party might win the Presidency. Hope flickered on in the darkening night.

One of Joe Johnston's own generals, the good and brave Pat Cleburne, worked out a proposal to strengthen the depleted armies. Use the Negroes, he suggested; train them, arm them, let them fight, give them freedom. Jefferson Davis suppressed this project, unsurprisingly. Ironically, early in 1865 the Confederate Congress would authorize the enrollment of slaves into the army—but it was too late; none ever fought.

Still another fresh tack was taken, to blast a hole in the blockade. Rebel ingenuity already had introduced floating mines, known as torpedoes, and small semisubmersible vessels that carried spar torpedoes, explosive warheads on long poles. Now the Confederacy looked to its submarine *H. L. Hunley,* third in a series of cigar-shaped "infernal machines." Sent out on the moonlit night of February 17 against the insolent blockaders at Charleston, trimmed just below the surface, she rammed a spar torpedo into the Union's new steam sloop *Housatonic.* With a muffled explosion her victim settled to the bottom; all but a handful of the crew were rescued. *Hunley* never returned. First submarine to sink a warship in combat, she had completed her last mission.

GOD KNOWS WHAT IS BEST for us, Robert E. Lee once wrote his wife. Sustained by such faith, he bore victory with humble gratitude and defeat with steadfast courage. Now, at 57, he was aging by the hour, stamped with the strain of war, hair and beard white, racked increasingly in his chest, back, and arms with paroxysms of pain.

It had been another cruel winter. "The weather is as cold as the world's charity," an Alabamian complained. During an inspection, he went on, he counted 31 men "who did not have a sign of a shoe on their feet." For two days Lee's soldiers received nothing to eat whatsoever.

I wonder what the general thought, studying his well-fed, well-equipped antagonist from the observation post on Clark's Mountain as spring turned the land green. Using fieldglasses, he scanned the Union host across the Rapidan. There waited "those people," as he nearly always called them, in their vast city of white tents on the rolling countryside near Culpeper, with flags fluttering, smoke of cookfires daubing ten thousand plumes on the sky, and the sweet notes of the bugle and peremptory rattle of the drum sounding softly on his ear.

Whatever pause this gave him, Lee feared not. "You must sometimes cast your thoughts on the Army of Northern Virginia," he told a relative, "and never forget it in your prayers. It is preparing for a great struggle, but I pray and trust that the great God, mighty to deliver, will spread over it His almighty arms, and drive its enemies before it."

Concealed Yankee patrol snipes at a party of Rebels. Important to both armies, these small bands ranged ahead of major units—often in contact with the enemy. Their minor but bitter fighting throughout the war inflicted many casualties.

DAVID G. BLYTHE, BEFORE 1865, BOSTON MUSEUM OF FINE ARTS, KAROLIK COLLECTION (ABOVE); MILITARY ORDER OF THE LOYAL LEGION, PHILADELPHIA

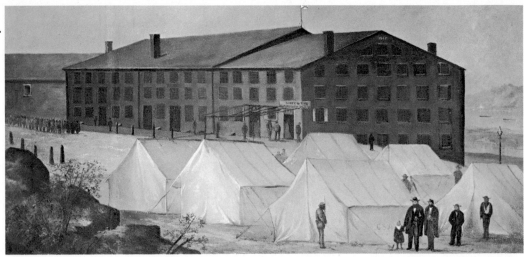

Now, Ulysses S. Grant didn't look at the matter in this light at all. He considered the conflict an unholy war, and the Confederacy's cause "one of the worst for which a people ever fought, and one for which there was the least excuse." Nor was U. S. Grant a man to be driven. He understood the science of war and made an art of it, which he termed simple enough. "Find out where your enemy is," he said, "get at him as soon as you can and strike him as hard as you can, and keep moving on."

The careworn Lincoln, who often simply sat on problems until they went away, admired his ruthless, hammering approach. He wanted Grant to keep moving on, keep moving on and end the war. On March 2 Grant had his third star. Lincoln promptly called him east to the Capitol and placed him at the head of all the armies of the United States.

Grant got down to work immediately. Good fighting weather drew near; he must be ready. For the first time, Federal forces everywhere would act together. East and West, they would strike the enemy in a simultaneous movement. In the cold and inexorable mathematics of war, Grant was setting the Union's superior military might into action.

In hard fact only two important Southern armies remained to be dealt with—Lee's in Virginia, Johnston's in Georgia. Grant gave General Sherman command of three armies in the West, and the two conferred in Cincinnati to work out details. Sherman later described in spare words the gist of that meeting: "He was to go for Lee, and I was to go for Joe Johnston. That was his plan." Destroy armed resistance, Grant held, and you destroy the Confederacy.

Simple enough in outline, but far from easy to do. George Meade, leading the Army of the Potomac, had not scored a major success against Robert Lee since the Battle of Gettysburg, ten months earlier. Yet Lee now mustered about 65,000 soldiers, at least 10,000 fewer than he fielded in Pennsylvania, while Meade's strength hovered around 120,000 troops, about 20,000 more than repulsed the Rebels on Cemetery Ridge and Little Round Top and the other bloody places.

Meade still commanded the army, but the new man from the West would direct it and the long rest was ending. The President looked at the odds and liked them. On April 30 he wrote Grant of his confidence in him and prayerfully sent him forth. "And now with a brave Army, and a just cause, may God sustain you," penned A. Lincoln.

Early in May the Union launched its concerted attack. Maj. Gen. Ben Butler, erstwhile scourge of New Orleans, now at Fort Monroe, was to land on the south bank of the James River and drive on Petersburg or Richmond, or both. He did neither, soon getting himself bottled up by the foe in a loop of the James. Maj. Gen. Nathaniel Banks, earlier a victim of Shenandoah inhospitality, was to move from New Orleans against Mobile, Alabama. Instead, he became hopelessly stuck in his futile Red River Campaign in Louisiana.

All side issues, these, important but not vital as things turned out. What mattered was that Sherman and more than 100,000 combative Yanks were advancing into northwest Georgia, and in Virginia Grant was crossing the Rapidan with more than 115,000 bluecoats, many regiments beginning their first active service. To the last soldier, it seemed, they were singing "John Brown's Body."

One veteran always remembered that mighty chorus in sorrow. "The

Despairing Union prisoners of war ignore a gesturing preacher in a symbolic painting of the Libby Prison in Richmond. A converted tobacco warehouse, the prison's tidy, well-scrubbed look (left) belied its stifling, vermin-infested interior. As the war progressed, prisons North and South became pestilential cages where thousands died of disease, hunger, and exposure.

wild, weird music . . . seems still resounding in my ears," he wrote, "and a feeling of sadness comes over me, when I think of the many voices which rang out on the balmy air . . . but which never sang again."

Had the war ever been so perverse, so contrary? Safely across the river, Grant struck southeast into the forbidding Wilderness. A year earlier almost to the day, Lee had outgeneraled Fighting Joe Hooker in and near this same devilish thicket. Grant hoped to get his wagon train — 70 miles long if filing down one road — out of the tangled country before Lee left his trenches. Then they could fight in the open.

Lee, of course, refused to cooperate. He plunged his columns into the Wilderness with a will, glad "those people" were locked in that gloomy jungle. The dense, brush-choked forest would neutralize the Union's greater numbers and render its excellent artillery almost useless. This would be a fierce fight in an endless maze.

What followed was a two-day battle, fought blind. The flash of muskets sometimes gave foemen away, but mostly bullets came singing out of nowhere and clipped leaves and branches from scrub oak and pine, sweet gum and cedar, and sent soldiers dangling limply over prickly vines and chinquapin bushes or sprawling beneath blooming dogwoods. Muzzle blasts set leaves ablaze, and the dry underbrush flamed up, woodsmoke adding to the confusion. Wounded soldiers screamed in terror as fire licked toward them; many screamed in vain.

"More desperate fighting has not been witnessed on this continent," Grant wrote with the weight of years on him, "than that of the 5th and 6th of May." Yet to him, crossing the Rapidan and getting his army together as a unit constituted a victory.

The battered Army of the Potomac hardly looked at it that way. Lee's determined Rebels stood there waiting for more, entrenched and inviting attack. They had lost an estimated 9,000 men. Grant had reported more than 17,000 casualties, and at best the thing was a standoff. Old-timers among the Federals figured that retreat would be called. Back

The Army of the Potomac sprawls to the horizon at Cumberland Landing on eastern

across the river they would rest and lick their wounds, just as in every campaign they had fought, and the war would never be finished.

Their march began as darkness deepened on May 7. Union divisions pulled out of the line and marched south—*south!*—curving past Lee's right flank, racing for a hamlet 10 miles distant named Spotsylvania Court House whose curse was that it rested on a strategic crossroads. If Grant reached it in time, he would be between Richmond and its defenders, and Lee would have to attack him head on. Grant rode toward the crossroads that night swiftly and silently. Along the road men recognized him, and cheered.

BUT LEE BEAT GRANT to Spotsylvania, and his men quickly dug themselves in. Bloodshed resumed. After breakfast on May 11, cigar in mouth, the Federal chieftain stepped into his tent, seated himself at his field table, and scrawled a dispatch to Washington. In it he reported heavy losses to date, perhaps 20,000; he thought the enemy's even higher and the result much in the Union's favor. "I . . . propose to fight it out on this line," he said, "if it takes all summer."

It would take much longer, and the line would continue to shift, but in that chance epigram Grant painted his own portrait and staked out two nations' future. Now he was General-in-Chief and the Civil War rested on his shoulders. He knew what he would do. Soldiers might fall like spring rain—others would replace them—that the Union might live.

The rank and file soon learned of Grant's fiat; newspapers reached camp blaring it. The pronouncement evoked no joy. A battle-toughened veteran—one who had "seen the elephant," in the slang of the times—summed it up in delicate mordancy: "We did not then appreciate the policy of attrition, and thought our lives as good as the rebels', man for man." In a month or so officers would be explaining confidentially why morning reports had not been called for. The country would not stand it, they agreed, if it knew the casualty figures.

Virginia's Pamunkey River. By 1864 this Federal juggernaut of 120,000 outnumbered Lee's forces nearly two to one.

JAMES HOPE, 1865, BOSTON MUSEUM OF FINE ARTS, KAROLIK COLLECTION

"The eyes of the Army," Lee called his dashing cavalry commander James E. B. *("Jeb") Stuart. Impetuous and egotistical, but magnificent in plumed hat and flowing red beard, Stuart forged Southern horsemen into a superb cavalry. On several occasions, they literally rode rings around the Army of the Potomac. When Stuart died on May 12, 1864, of a wound he received at Yellow Tavern, near Richmond, Lee pronounced a simple tribute: "He never brought me a piece of false information." At right, his saddle, gloves, and a saddlebag lie on a length of Confederate uniform cloth. He remains a gallant symbol of a dying but tenacious Confederacy that made up in courage what it lacked in numbers. Early in May the two armies tangled once again in the Wilderness, the first of 1864's major battles. The Union lost almost 18,000 men but, instead of retreating, sidestepped south toward Richmond. Lee hurried to head off the Yankees at Spotsylvania.*

A fine horseman himself, Grant knew well that attrition could be produced by cavalry no less than infantry. Slight, pugnacious Maj. Gen. Philip H. Sheridan, spectacular fighter at Missionary Ridge, took over the Army of the Potomac's troopers. The new General-in-Chief picked acid-tongued "Little Phil" for the job; both believed in all-out, never-ease-up, let's-get-on-with-it warfare.

On the day that Grant forwarded his blunt dispatch to Washington, Sheridan and 10,000 horsemen neared Richmond's outskirts expecting to find the city under attack by Ben Butler. Instead, they found a scrap with James Ewell Brown Stuart. Cape billowing, he rode with 3,200 Rebels to challenge the Federals in the fields around a roadside haven named Yellow Tavern, and received a mortal wound. Little Phil and company departed.

Stuart's comrades sent him into Richmond, into a private home where Jefferson Davis came to say farewell. His wife did not arrive before the end. He wanted to hear "Rock of Ages, cleft for me," and someone sang it. That was all for the last cavalier.

When Jeb Stuart fell, I think, the Old South was laid to rest in glory. In truth, he died an anachronism, as did the society he fought for. Little remained but courage. . . . Down to the present one senses that courage, and respects it. One also finds, without difficulty, the Old South's ghostly ambiance drifting through the villages and backcountry, and one sometimes comes upon it lingering in the quiet and exclusive parlors of the bustling cities.

Back when the war was young and hearts were high, Abraham Lincoln had called for 75,000 militia to serve 90 days and suppress "combinations too powerful" for the ordinary process of law. The time came when, in wry humor, he refused a man a pass through the lines to Richmond: "I would gladly give you the pass if it would do any good, but in the last two years I have given passes to Richmond to 250,000 men and not one of them managed to get there yet."

Surely the god of battles was frowning on U. S. Grant. In the Wilderness he had held the advantage briefly; followed up, he said, it must have proved very decisive. Next, by arriving first at Spotsylvania Court House, he would have turned Lee's flank; he arrived just too late.

At Spotsylvania, Grant almost—almost—cut the Army of Northern Virginia in half. On May 10 his men briefly forced their way into the "Mule Shoe," a U-shaped salient bulging from the Confederate lines. On the 12th he cracked it, said a Southerner, "as the rail-splitter's wedge rives the timber as it is driven into the narrow crack." The Federals rushed through; Lee, seeing the danger, resolved to lead the counterattack in person. The men who would give their lives would not risk his. They grabbed Traveller by the bridle and turned him around, crying "General Lee to the rear!" Not until he was safe would they fight. Then they drove the Yankees back.

For more than 16 hours the incredible soldiers of both sides wrestled to the death in violent rainsqualls for a point famed thereafter as the Bloody Angle. No more furious combat surged anywhere in all the war. Here they fired point-blank, skewered one another with bayonet, clubbed one another down with musket butt. Dead and wounded men piled up in heaps; the living fought on top of them, grinding them into the muck and burying some alive. In the end, Lee's line was safe.

At Cold Harbor Grant tried again. On June 1 he tackled part of the well-fortified Rebel line head on and lost 1,500 troops. A less obdurate, one might almost say less bullheaded, general would have concluded that this was not the way to get at Lee, and tried maneuvering. Not Grant. He ordered a frontal assault on June 3 against the six-mile Confederate line. Men looked at the formidable trenches they must storm, wrote their names on pieces of paper and pinned them to their blouses; no point to dying namelessly. Then they charged, in what has been called "the most awful thirty minutes known to the Union Army."

Maj. Gen. George Pickett, CSA, never the same after Gettysburg but still trying, watched the bluecoats come. "The whole Confederate line poured a stream of fire," he said, "and thousands of Grant's soldiers have gone to reenforce the army of the dead." Being Pickett, he could see from this terrible sight to the sad futility beyond it—"Oh, this is all a weary, long mistake."

The immediate mistake belonged to Grant, and it cost the North about 7,000 men. Lee's casualties came to around 1,500. The Union general in his memoirs said the least he could: "I have always regretted that the last assault at Cold Harbor was ever made."

Robert E. Lee won a clear victory there, though a defensive one. He would never win another in the field. He could not replace his losses. He could hold; he could not attack.

Grant owned the initiative, although he had manpower problems himself. Thousands of his best combat soldiers, their three years of volunteer service over, were leaving the army. Replacements ranged from sound troops new to the battlefield to semiworthless "bounty men." For a while in May, Lee got more reinforcements than Grant; in that month of unrelieved, bitter, valiant warfare, the Union lost about as many soldiers as the Confederacy had started with. Fifty thousand. Nevertheless, sooner or later, Grant would grind Lee down.

Horribly repulsed at Cold Harbor, Grant slipped away from Lee's

Sturdy oak cut down by bullets attests the fury of the fighting at Bloody Angle, where a Union assault almost wrecked the Confederate line around Spotsylvania Court House. Quitting the bloodied Wilderness, Rebels and Yankees contested the square mile of territory (right) on May 12 in a day of ferocious combat.

*The Last Campaign: In the
spring of 1864, the Federal
Army of the Potomac and Lee's
Army of Northern Virginia
bumped and jostled each other
across eastern Virginia, grap-
pling in major battles at the
Wilderness, Spotsylvania, the
North Anna, and Cold Harbor.
Bluffing Lee at Riddell's Shop,
Grant swept wide around him,
crossed the James, and laid siege
to Petersburg. A month and a
half of fighting cost the North
60,000 men, the South 30,000.*

front after dark on June 12, again moving to the left—southeast. Crossing the James River over a swiftly laid pontoon bridge, he headed for
the vital rail junction of Petersburg. Richmond and the Army of Northern Virginia depended for their lives on the food and supplies, scant as
they were, brought by train—primarily from the Valley. Nearly all the
trains came through Petersburg, 25 miles below the Rebel Capital.

Here too it could have ended, and should have. Petersburg was so
lightly defended when the Union's leading elements came up that a
firm assault must have carried the town in short order. Inept forward
leadership prevailed, instead; Beauregard led a defense of desperation
and Lee's tatterdemalion stalwarts arrived in time to secure the lines.

Grant now would dig in, tear up the railroads, and starve out the
Army of Northern Virginia. Lee had forecast a siege if Grant crossed
the James; "then," he predicted, "it will be a mere question of time."

The question turned on time in Georgia, too, and there wily Joe
Johnston played the waiting game. Outmanned and outgunned, why
should he make gimlet-eyed Sherman happy by risking all in open
battle? He chose to dally behind stout earthworks and wink invitingly
at the Federals; one combat-wise Reb in the line equaled three or four
Yankees in the attack.

The edgy, sharp-minded Sherman knew this formula well, and he
wasn't about to go for Johnston as Grant had been going for Lee. He
attracted Johnston's attention with Thomas's army while trying to flank
him with one of the others. Naturally, the Confederate general refused
to stand still for this and kept dancing sideways as a partner should.
His skill and Sherman's inspire soldiers to this day.

Beginning early in May, the mutually respectful enemies one-stepped
from the vicinity of Dalton in northwest Georgia south about a hundred
miles, arriving on Atlanta's outskirts two months later. Hard fighting
did occur along the way, of course. Even today some of the old earthworks at the town of Resaca still rise, innocent hillocks overlooking
Interstate 75. Nearly 60 miles south at New Hope Church, one needs
only a good guide while walking over that bloodied ground to feel the
fury that flared up in the four-day engagement there.

And around Kennesaw Mountain, where Sherman finally *did* test the
capable Johnston head on, I could see clearly why he received so fearful
a rebuke. Determined Confederates had created a fortress on the slopes
and crest, soldiers dragging heavy cannon up tortuous trails too steep
for horses. When men in blue charged at Kennesaw on June 27, men in
gray coolly squinted down their musket sights. The hail of lead flattened
about 2,500 Federals before "Uncle Billy" backed off.

Next day, a young Ohioan sat down on the ground and wrote his
family about that hell, using a hardtack box as a desk. He could hear a
"batery of artilery" firing. He spoke of "considerable loss," and he had a
presentiment. As he talked about what it would be like to come home,
his immediate situation flashed to mind with the suddenness of a Minié
ball: ". . . if I am spared through the campaign." Prospects didn't seem
too bright, but one thing brought comfort: "I think that if I ever geet
home again I will apriciate religious things more. . . ."

My youthful great-uncle Leonidas Jordan composed those words.
Back in mid-'62 he had received a medical discharge for typhoid, the

159

army doctor finding him unfit for further service. Yet here he sat on a blood-drenched field in Georgia, 19 years old now and half a head taller than the chipper lad of 17 who chased Stonewall Jackson in the Shenandoah Valley until "Old Jack" captured and paroled him.

I think I know why Private Jordan, Company G, 31st Ohio Veteran Volunteer Infantry, signed up again. Beyond patriotism, of which he had plenty, lay another consideration. The $300 bounty he received for re-enlisting, and his meager army pay, would help provide for his invalid father, mother, and seven younger brothers and sisters. It was the best he could do, in any event. When his father died, not long before the fighting at Kennesaw Mountain, Leonidas set down his simple faith: "If I was to go home," he wrote his mother, "I would kind of expect to see Pap but it can not bee so we must try and bee reconciled to the will of an all wise god."

Such men fought the Civil War for Union and Confederacy alike, and the war dragged on in Georgia as in Virginia. Pitched battle at Kennesaw, sharp clashes here and there, endless marching and maneuvering —slowly Northerners and Southerners sidled toward Atlanta.

Among the unsung heroes along the way walked the skirmishers, the men out front who kept in touch. Only the atmosphere separated a thin line of advancing skirmishers from the entrenched enemy. Halting finally, almost within spitting distance, some riflemen would try to pin the foe down with their fire while others frantically dug "gopher holes" with axes, picks, and shovels, or—lacking these—bare hands. Each pit, 8 or 10 feet long, would harbor three or four soldiers.

The foot soldier's war ground on in Georgia, inglorious but moving toward a dim yet increasingly sensed end. "I think that all that do geet home," remarked Private Jordan, "will bee home before very much longer." On July 17 Jefferson Davis decided he'd seen enough of Joe Johnston's tactics and fired him. Sherman was pounding at Atlanta's door, Davis reckoned, because Johnston hadn't brought him to battle; loss of the city's industries and railroads would damage the Confederacy

Plotting his next move, Grant studies a map at his Cold Harbor headquarters, his dedicated Chief of Staff John A. Rawlins seated beside him. In the gravest mistake of his military career, Grant had ordered an assault at Cold Harbor on June 3 against impregnable Rebel trenches, costing the Union 7,000 men in about half an hour. Infantrymen like those below faced deadly fire. Forsaking such bludgeoning tactics, Grant swung toward Petersburg.

irreparably. Besides, the President disliked the touchy, proud general.

Davis wanted somebody to smash Sherman. He handed over command of the army, to its great dismay, to rash, one-legged John Bell Hood. Riding strapped to his horse, General Hood would attack, right enough; he would attack until nothing was left to attack with.

Col. Allen P. Julian, USA (Ret.), of Atlanta, eminent historian of Georgia's role in the Civil War, conducted me over many of the state's battlefields. Only three days after Johnston was relieved, he noted, the new commander mounted a direct assault at Peachtree Creek, on the city's northern outskirts, and Sherman sternly repulsed him. On July 22, he savagely attacked on its east side in what became known as the Battle of Atlanta, and the Federals forced him to retire into his strong fortifications. A few days later, on the west side at Ezra Church, Hood tried a fresh assault, fruitlessly.

BETWEEN BATTLES, Ned Julian recalled, a Union picket struck up a conversation with his Confederate counterpart. "Well, Johnny," said the cocky Yank, "how many of you are left?" Johnny, member of an infantry unsurpassed in courage and tenacity, knew Hood's grim toll. "Oh," he answered, still game, "about enough for another killing."

Pickets and skirmishers of each side often arranged truces between fighting. Small knots of Yanks and Johnnies played poker and twenty-one inside the lines while other Federals swapped coffee, salt, and pepper for anything a poor Reb could offer. During one such social, Union orders came to begin firing when the bugle blew. Trading and card-playing continued until one of the bluecoats yelled, "Hunt your holes, Johnnies!" and everyone dived for cover. Northern men opened a brisk fire; Southerners responded with vigor. When the musketry slackened, a Confederate called out, "Is that all, Yanks?" Assured that it was, open house resumed in no man's land.

My great-uncle took pen in hand during one of these free times, observing that the boys were trading for tobacco and "such thing." The insanity of it all hit him, and he thought back to "right smart of a fight" on the preceding Sunday. His description must have struck terror into his widowed mother's heart, although I am sure he did not realize it:

"We wer out one picket and they advanced on us but we would not drive worth a cent we lost twenty seven in killed and wounded we had our orderly sargeant killed he was shot through the heart their was two of the rosevill boys wounded one of home I expect will lose his arm we also lost our captain he was shot in the mouth it kict his teeth out but luckly the ball was spent I was out on vidett ahead of the regiment I tell you what they mad mee geet back in a hury . . . the company is getting down to its usual number we have now thirty eight men out of eighty eight when we started. . . ."

I have been able to pinpoint that clash. It occurred early in August on Atlanta's southwest side, one of several encounters in the rolling land around Utoy Creek. "Uncle Billy" Sherman told Washington in a dispatch that it amounted to a "noisy but not a bloody battle."

From his perspective, it was just another step in the effort to get at Hood and take Atlanta. He was besieging the city now, bombarding it daily, killing such civilians as his shells found and giving the volunteer

Negro troops assault the broken Rebel line around Petersburg in the Battle of the Crater. Halted by earthworks before the city, Grant laid siege in mid-June. He authorized a regiment made up largely of Pennsylvania coal miners to tunnel under the Rebel fortifications. There they planted 8,000 pounds of black powder and blasted a gap 170 feet wide in the Southern line. But bungling Yankee officers failed to exploit the advantage, missing the chance to take the city and sever Lee's army. Alfred R. Waud (left), photographed earlier by one of Brady's assistants, sketched the action, whimsically adding enormous feet to the last soldier.

fire department much employment. In the same dispatch, Sherman noted that whether he got inside Atlanta or not, one thing was certain — it would be a used-up community when he finished with it.

The tough encircling defenses of this industrial and transportation center might have tempted a general early in the war, but Sherman wanted no part of them. He swung around, cutting railroads one by one, leaving his mark all the way. Ripping up track, his men heated rails red-hot in the fires of burning ties and then twisted them around trees. "Sherman's neckties," troops called them.

Late in August the Union general wheeled southwest around the city to Jonesboro on the Macon & Western Central, and Hood came out to attack him, for this was his army's last supply line. He slammed into the Federals, failed, and evacuated Atlanta. Sherman walked in.

While Sherman had been working his way toward Atlanta and Grant was hacking his bloody path to Petersburg, Lincoln was buffeted by criticism as never before. He had failed to put down the rebellion after three agonizing years, and the casualty lists were horrifying. To make matters worse, Lt. Gen. Jubal Early and around 10,000 Confederates, having swept the Shenandoah Valley clean of Federal forces, had marched into Maryland and on July 11 arrived in front of Fort Stevens — less than an hour's carriage ride from the White House.

Once again Washington quaked. Grant had rushed thousands of soldiers to defend the Capital; Lincoln met veterans from Petersburg as they disembarked at the Potomac wharves. They soon filled Fort Stevens' defenses, and the experienced Early knew what he was up against. After two days of minor fighting at the fort — while Lincoln stood among the bullets and watched — "Old Jube" retreated to Virginia.

The President's hope for re-election waned; he desperately needed convincing victories. After August 5 he took heart a little. Starchy old Rear Adm. David Glasgow Farragut, a sea dog since 1811, steamed into Mobile Bay, cried (according to legend) "Damn the torpedoes! Full steam ahead!" when a Confederate mine sank one of his 18 ships, and took the most essential Rebel port on the Gulf of Mexico.

It helped, but it wasn't enough. Lincoln was convinced that the November election would decide whether the Union would fight on or give up, and he grew profoundly pessimistic. On August 23 he wrote a memorandum and pigeonholed it for further use: "This morning, as for some days past, it seems exceedingly probable that this Administration will not be re-elected. Then it will be my duty to so co-operate with the President elect, as to save the Union between the election and the inauguration; as he will have secured his election on such ground that he can not possibly save it afterwards."

But after September 2, when Sherman entered Atlanta, the North's despondency evaporated like mist in the morning sun. An elated Lincoln had the good news he needed. Retired General McClellan, running on a peace platform and war talk, would carry only New Jersey, Delaware, and Kentucky. Lincoln would be the man for the people.

Toward the end of September, Little Phil Sheridan gave the North another victory. General Early was prowling the Shenandoah, and that fertile mountain-sheltered land served as Lee's main storehouse. Grant ordered Sheridan to follow Early to the death. The riproaring Federal

Short, dumpy, and deadly, the "Dictator" squats on a railroad car outside Petersburg. During the 10-month siege of the city, the 17,000-pound mortar lobbed 200-pound exploding shells on Rebel entrenchments. Defending troops could see the burning fuses at night and soon learned to dodge the missiles. At left, three young visitors at Petersburg National Battlefield rest on a concrete model of the "Dictator" and listen to a guitarist.

Sailors scramble aboard a lifeboat as C.S.S. Alabama *goes down after a pummeling by U.S.S.* Kearsarge *off Cherbourg, France, on June 19, 1864. The private yacht* Deerhound *(left) steams*

in to help pick up survivors. The loss of the Alabama, *a highly successful cruiser that sank, burned, or captured 69 prizes in 11 months, left the Confederacy's pitifully weak navy even more ineffective.*

cavalryman ultimately drove him out of the Valley and devastated it. Sheridan and Grant spoke of this work in the same terms: A crow would have had to carry its rations if it had flown across the Valley.

It still remained for Grant and Lee to fight it out, and pugnacious Hood still demanded Sherman's attention. At the same time, Sherman was converting Atlanta into a military garrison; civilians had to leave. Contacted by letter, Hood agreed to help convey the refugees south, but he protested bitterly: "And now, sir," he wrote Sherman, "permit me to say that the unprecedented measure you propose transcends, in studied and ingenious cruelty, all acts ever before brought to my attention in the dark history of war."

This kicked off a vituperative exchange in which neither commander yielded an iota. The Union leader, a gifted writer, *did* soften his tone, but otherwise remained adamant, when Atlanta city officials petitioned him to reconsider. "You cannot qualify war in harsher terms than I will," replied Sherman. "War is cruelty, and you cannot refine it.... You might as well appeal against the thunder-storm as against these terrible hardships of war."

How must the unhappy supplicants have felt, their city a shambles and their people ordered out, young, old, sick and well alike, when the general assured them of his compassion? "But, my dear sirs, when peace does come, you may call on me for any thing. Then will I share with you the last cracker, and watch with you to shield your homes and families against danger from every quarter...."

Crackers and other supplies undoubtedly preoccupied "Uncle Billy" as he bade Atlanta farewell. The army's food and supplies rolled by rail all the way from Louisville through Nashville and Chattanooga to

Tough, tenacious Maj. Gen. William Tecumseh Sherman, a prophet of total war, attacked the mind of the South, crippling the Confederacy's will to fight. While Grant kept Lee busy in Virginia, Sherman advanced from Tennessee toward Atlanta. On July 22 his men battled Rebel defenders along the Georgia Railroad (below) with the skyline of the doomed city visible in the distance.

With Sherman on the outskirts, Confederate
casualties of the Battle of Atlanta wait in the railroad
yard for transportation south in a scene from the
epic film *Gone With the Wind.* The heroine,
Scarlett O'Hara (left), steps among the wounded.

Atlanta, nearly 500 miles. South from Nashville, 16 trains of 10 cars ran daily, carrying 1,600 tons of matériel and making 10 miles an hour. This single-track line presented an obvious target for General Hood, and that indomitable gentleman raced northwest to strike at it. Sherman left a corps to guard Atlanta and chased after him. By mid-October Hood was retreating into northeast Alabama.

Part of his haggard command trudged through Snake Creek Gap, a wild and gloomy slash in the low mountains west of Resaca. Guided by my Atlanta friend Colonel Julian, I made a kind of pilgrimage to Snake Creek Gap. The 31st Ohio, with Leonidas Jordan present for duty, skirmished with Hood's rear guard through this picturesque defile. It remains unchanged, said Ned Julian, except that the old dirt road has been paved. High, tree-veiled ridges rise on either side; towering pines shutter the narrow gorge, and sometimes sunlight penetrates only briefly. It wasn't a comfortable place, I thought; the Rebels made it worse in their day by felling trees to obstruct it.

Working through, the 31st observed that stalks of sugar cane, chewed to pulp, littered the abandoned enemy camps; Johnny was short on rations. The Ohio boys may have been a little hungry themselves; they sent out a foraging party and Private Jordan went along.

Foraging, like skirmishing and picketing, was dangerous. At this late juncture of the war bands of murderous bushwhackers lurked on the fringes of marching armies, preying on innocent people already swamped in the conflict. Riffraff and deserters from both sides joined these bands. If they surprised army scouts or foragers, they killed without mercy, robbed and disposed of the bodies, and fled.

Somewhere in Snake Creek Gap's reaches, bushwhackers got the drop on Leonidas and his brave and miserable war came to an end. I wonder how they took him. Did they shoot him dead from their forest cover? That would have been best. Did they take him alive and taunt him? Did they have some sport and hang him?

I don't know. Records in the National Archives mention the bushwhackers but are certain only of this: When his buddies searched for him, all they found was his gun and knapsack; he was never seen again. Grateful for Leonidas Jordan's service, the Government awarded his mother $8 a month.

With the energy of desperation, Hood decided to strike into Tennessee. Sherman might follow him, he figured, evacuating Atlanta at least; but even if he didn't, the Confederate army could whip Union forces in Tennessee and, resupplying at Nashville, march up through Kentucky and menace Ohio. Thus, he hoped, it would be a brand new war.

Hood pointed his long-suffering Southerners north—and Sherman headed his much-walked Northerners south: two opposing armies turning their backs on each other. Actually, Hood probably was doing the best thing he could, and Sherman was possessed and driven by a great and terrible dream.

Sherman had satisfied himself and Grant that Pap Thomas, the Rock of Chickamauga, would have enough Federals in Tennessee to cope with Hood. On November 12 he broke his railroad and telegraph communications, rendering him completely out of touch with the Union. Three days later he burned Atlanta's war industries and stepped off for Savannah and the sea. He would live off the land and "make Georgia howl," severing the Deep South east and west, displaying its defenselessness, showing all Confederates the folly of their ways.

Total war, 1864. More than 60,000 Federals headed south that bracing morning, muskets gleaming in the sun, and a pall of black smoke hung over the city they left. A band struck up "John Brown's Body." Soldiers lifted their voices, thrilling their commander. "Glory, glory, Hallelujah!" never sounded better to him.

I think I know U. S. Grant. William Tecumseh Sherman proves far more complex. How should one regard him? Here, in my view, stood a brilliant soldier who took peculiar zest in destroying civilian property as well as his armed enemy. Here, looming even more frightful, roared a self-appointed avenger sweeping down in righteous wrath—but it was helpless men, women, and children he drove from their homes, maintaining he did them a kindness. Here strode a conqueror who, marching almost unopposed to the sea, scorched the earth and closed his eyes to the inevitable plundering. Is this the stuff of greatness?

YET SHERMAN EMERGES larger than all this. The South's capacity and will to make war posed a legitimate target; the sooner he smashed them, the sooner peace would come. Thinking of his own children, he devoted himself to that ideal: peace. He looked with a seer's vision far beyond the pall he raised over Georgia to a reunited land of a common glory . . . to a reborn United States. Then there would be forgiveness under the "old flag"—the Stars and Stripes—of the mighty Union.

Georgia howled. Endless lines of Federals tramped down her red-earth roads in four roughly parallel columns, hiking 10 or 15 miles a day and picking clean an area up to 60 miles wide. They confiscated or destroyed anything that aided the Confederacy's military effort, ripping up railroads, burning bridges and factories, emptying arsenals, and ruining machine shops.

Setting forth every morning, foragers scoured the countryside and returned with wagons groaning under the weight of hams, bacon, poultry, cornmeal, sweet corn, sweet potatoes, beans, molasses, and other items. Cattle accompanied them in great numbers. Soldiers dined sumptuously. In fact, they obtained much more food than they needed, but that was the idea: Strip the land, prevent Rebel armies from getting enough to eat. Too bad that women and children went hungry. Some of the surplus was given to the growing ranks of Negroes that flocked behind. The remainder rotted.

While the devil-may-care Yankees marched through Georgia, Hood and his courageous rabble pushed north in Tennessee, lashed by rain, sleet, snow, and freezing cold as November grew old. At Spring Hill they hoped to cut off a 22,000-man Union force led by Maj. Gen. John M. Schofield, a balding, long-bearded West Point classmate of Hood. To the latter's chagrin, Schofield slipped away and escaped to the nearby town of Franklin where he took refuge in strong fortifications. Enraged, Hood pursued on the double, arriving at the hamlet's southern edge about midafternoon on November 30.

I wanted to see that storied field, and Stanley F. Horn of Nashville, the widely known Civil War historian and *Continued on page 178*

Ripping up railroads, destroying bridges, and foraging liberally, Sherman's men plunder anything that might aid the Rebels. On November 15, after occupying Atlanta for ten weeks, Sherman left on his march to the sea. As he advanced

*virtually unopposed—raking a band of desolation 60 miles wide across the state
—Southerners boiled in helpless rage. Reaching the coast in December, he wired
Lincoln: "I beg to present you as a Christmas-gift the city of Savannah...."*

175

LITHOGRAPH (BELOW) AFTER THURE DE THULSTRUP, 1885, COURTESY FORT WARD MUSEUM, ALEXANDRIA, VIRGINIA, LORD COLLECTION; THOMAS ANTHONY DEFEO

Fertile Shenandoah Valley, a major source of food for Lee's army, sprawls across northwestern Virginia. As 1864's summer waned—with stalemate at Petersburg, siege at Atlanta—Maj. Gen. Philip H. Sheridan received orders to lay waste the Valley and drive out Jubal Early's Rebel force. Archibald Rowand, reporting to Sheridan (right), served him as a scout. At left, his cavalry routs the enemy at Winchester on September 19. A month later to the day, "Old Jube" struck back at Cedar Creek; but "Little Phil," galloping 14 miles in a furious ride from Winchester, rallied his scattered men and reversed the retreat as he went. That counterassault spelled the beginning of the end for Early and the beginning of a legend for Sheridan.

author, drove me there. Mr. Horn believes that Pickett's famed charge at Gettysburg fades into the shadows when compared to what happened at Franklin. I think he may very well be right.

Hood paid no heed to the Federals' powerful position. He must attack. Eighteen thousand soldiers formed in battle array on a front two miles wide, advanced in perfect order across two miles of open fields, came on steadily in the face of scythe-like shot and shell, assaulted desperately time and again, fought into the night and neither won nor lost but did not quit the field...and more than 6,000 valiant Confederates dropped, among them 12 generals—five killed outright, a sixth mortally wounded, five more wounded, one captured.

Next day, Mr. Horn told me, corpses were found standing in the trenches, supported by dead comrades heaped as many as seven deep. A Rebel who lived through it rose from the gory field at dawn, and looked about unbelievingly; he called it the grand coronation of death.

Schofield received nearly 2,500 casualties. During the night he withdrew about 18 miles north to Nashville's defenses, augmenting the large Union force already there under General Thomas. Hood followed with his gallant barefoot troops. Entrenching in the hills south of the city, he waited, seeking an opening; if he could repulse a Federal attack, Nashville might be won.

But Pap Thomas came out on December 15 and crushed Hood's left wing in an excellently planned, well-executed attack. Mr. Horn quoted an old military maxim: "The passive defense is a form of deferred suicide." When Hood was routed at Nashville, the historian said, it sealed the Confederacy's fate: "This was the Waterloo of the war."

A few days later the despairing South got more bad news. Sherman entered Savannah, his march to the sea a triumph. Jauntily he telegraphed President Lincoln: "I beg to present you as a Christmas-gift the city of Savannah...."

Facing a battle for re-election, Lincoln poses in 1864 in Brady's studio for this "most satisfactory likeness," according to his son Robert. Today it appears on our $5 bills. Below, General Sheridan casts his ballot in the field. Like most Yankee veterans, he voted for Lincoln and the Union, repudiating the platform of the Democrats calling for immediate peace. Victories at Atlanta and in the Shenandoah assured Lincoln a second term.

1865:
AN END AND A BEGINNING

CHAPTER SIX

NOT LONG AFTER the final year opened, Mary Boykin Chesnut—whose husband had gone to serve with the death-thinned forces of the South—noted in her diary that a friend had come to call. As they chatted, her maid burst into "Massa's in de cold, cold ground." The lyric struck a nerve. "Stop, Ellen!" she cried. "Sing something else!"

"Well," her friend spoke up, "most of them are."

Today, contemplating the Civil War's grim canvas as 1865 arrives, one sees that the portrait requires very little to be complete. Nearly four years earlier, Southerners had exercised their right to make a revolution. Their Northern brothers objected and took to the sword, plunging the land into Stygian horror. Daylight broke through as 1864's fury died, clearly revealing a defeated and bankrupt Confederacy.

No real options existed, merely delusions. Only one path could be followed. It rolled from Atlantic to Pacific over fields green with promise and prairies unplowed and mountains to be conquered and deserts waiting to bloom. The way had always been there, banding a continent in the ancient scheme of things, ranging wide and far across the United States of America. Now all Americans, North and South, black and white, must take that path and the course of Union in freedom.

The tragedy was over, finished, and the last soldier should have fallen, but he hadn't. The grisly wringer continued to turn; the conflict would burn itself out at a certain time and place, neither quite to hand. That had long since been established. If the Union had scored a crushing victory at the First Battle of Bull Run, perhaps—*perhaps*—the rebellion would have ended then.

In 1862 a saber's slash might—*might*—have secured that single decisive victory: Bragg's invasion of Kentucky, Lee's invasion of Maryland. . . . By the end of that year no such chance remained. If the will would endure, strength would prevail. Which simply meant that every man, woman, and child in this land from then to now and into tomorrow would win the Civil War, and lose it too. The evidence rests all about us today.

Years before the war began, thoughtful men saw it coming and predicted its outcome. Early in the struggle itself, in 1862 when autumn's benign sun warmed tawny fields around a Maryland village named Sharpsburg and soldiers' blood tinted Antietam Creek, people of both sections heard distant bells toll for the Confederacy. On Independence Day of 1863, when hundreds of Southerners sprawled in violent death's indignity on Gettysburg's alien field, and when triumphant Northern regiments trooped into battered, starving Vicksburg, the muffled drums of doom beat more insistently.

As 1864 departed, Confederate hopes faded like the haunting echoes

Union drummer boy summons his comrades from their quarters in a bleak, snow-dusted camp. In the decisive winter of 1865, drummers in blue sounded calls for an army quickened by the sweeping victories of Sherman and Sheridan and now destined to triumph over the crumbling Confederacy when spring had come to Appomattox.

Confederate riflemen and cannoneers fiercely but vainly defend Fort Fisher, January 15, 1865, against the overwhelming force of naval bombardment, invasion by sailors and Marines and an

infantry attack. Capture of the South's most forbidding coastal citadel sealed the harbor of Wilmington, North Carolina — last haven for blockade-runners — and cut off the Rebels' vital seaborne supplies. 183

of Taps, that Civil War bugle requiem whose dying notes still send soldiers to repose. Atlanta smoldered; the Deep South lay prostrate; Nashville bore mute testimony to a last, foolhardy, valiant Rebel might-have-been, smashed into the snow, silent now as stilled cannon and young men asleep in shallow graves.

The proof was in and it was conclusive. Yet bloodshed continued: Soldiers die easily; war dies hard. This carnival of death died hard because of outsize humans like Abraham Lincoln and U. S. Grant, Jefferson Davis and Robert E. Lee, each in his own person standing for or against a way of life that was growing from the ashes of another. If one says only that Grant and Lee were soldiers, one says enough.

Jeff Davis and Abe Lincoln also manifested something in common: resolution. Davis, whiplashed by critics, deep lines scribed in his face, sick and weary, held unwaveringly to his faith in the cause. In his mind, he and the cause were one and the same. This tragic figure sat in his Richmond office approving and disapproving the assignment of clerks as well as matters of state, as if his domain had not shrunk to parts of North and South Carolina, a fraction of Virginia, the isolated trans-Mississippi enclave, and pockets elsewhere. We must fight on, he implored. And Lee the soldier obeyed, doing his duty.

NO LESS THAN DAVIS DID LINCOLN — Father Abraham, Old Abe — feel the struggle's crushing burden. Sorrow bone-deep in him, compassion lighting his eyes, he too held steadfast: The Union must be preserved, the black man free. He would die for these principles, first soldier of them all, and his time drew near, as did the Confederacy's. The one eventuality shimmered in the obsessed brain of an actor named John Wilkes Booth; the other already loomed up as palpable as truth itself, like something you bump your nose on.

Dirty, crowded, rundown, freezing Richmond itself forecast the end. Most men who could had shipped their women and children away long since; here and there congenial areas still existed in the South. About mid-January, as the last major Confederate port — Wilmington, North Carolina — closed with the fall of Fort Fisher, a barrel of flour cost $1,250. Pigeons, mice, and most rats had disappeared; around hospitals, where rats got enough to eat, male nurses and orderlies found them tasty, planked and broiled. The dollar's value kept dwindling; on January 19, $70 Confederate bought $1 in gold. A slave who was worth at least $1,000 before the war now sold for $100 gold; soon someone would trade a Negro for a keg of nails.

Bitter weather also plagued the Confederate Capital's denizens. A man might scrape up $80 to buy a bushel of corn meal and get enough mush inside him to quell a mutinous stomach, but then he could turn pockets inside out searching for $100 to purchase a load of wood or coal for his frigid room. More than 100,000 crammed the dismal city, cellar to garret — government workers, toilers in munitions plants, ordnance shops, and uniform factories, refugees, wounded and sick soldiers, deserters, speculators, and all kinds of human derelicts and the dregs of war. Everybody shivered and tightened belts and waited, and some doubtless took strength from the minister's text one Sunday: "Why are ye fearful, O ye of little faith?" *Continued on page 190*

Confederate conqueror of Fort Sumter at the war's outset, Gen. P. G. T. Beauregard forfeited the stronghold to Union troops on February 17, 1865; forced out by Sherman, he ordered Charleston evacuated. Four days later, Negroes of the 55th Massachusetts Infantry Regiment marched down Broad Street in the oft-

bombarded seat of rebellion. Their triumphant rendition of "John Brown's March" mingled with the joyous shouts of Charleston's liberated slaves. One of the officers reported: "The white population remained within their houses, but curiosity led even them to peep through the blinds at the 'black Yankees.'"

Alexander H. Stephens (left), Vice President of the Confederacy, proposed unacceptable peace terms to Lincoln, February 3, aboard the River Queen off Fort Monroe at Hampton Roads, Virginia. Although eager for war's end, the President sought peace for "the people of our one common country" and could never accept the Confederate demand for independence. In late March, on the same steamer anchored upriver at City Point, Lincoln received Sherman, Grant, and Admiral Porter to discuss plans on how best to bring the grueling, gory conflict between the states to a conclusion. His generals warned him that peace would require "one more bloody battle, and that it would be the last."

Union stronghold in Confederate territory, moated Fort Monroe became Jefferson Davis's prison in May 1865. As a young

G. P. A. HEALY, C. 1868, THE WHITE HOUSE (ABOVE); J. BAYLOR ROBERTS

officer, Lee had served a tour of duty here, and Monitor *and* Merrimack *engaged in their celebrated duel nearby.*

Union-held Fort Sedgwick, focal point for converging fire of Confederate batteries, acquired the nickname "Fort Hell" during the 10-month siege of Petersburg. Only 600 yards separated it from Rebel Fort Mahone, known as "Fort Damnation." Typically, the crude redoubt included chevaux-de-frise, sharpened stakes embedded in logs to discourage direct assault (upper left); and gabions, wickerware bundles, and log revetments used as retaining walls. Troops quartered in mud-and-log huts endured great hardship here until Grant's successes forced the fall of Petersburg, supply depot for tottering Richmond. After Union victories, many captured Rebels preferred the scorn of their comrades to imprisonment and, taking the oath of allegiance to the United States, donned Federal uniforms.

NATIONAL ARCHIVES (ABOVE); FRANK LESLIE'S ILLUSTRATED NEWSPAPER, 1864

Placid Five Forks shook with battle thunder on April 1 when Sheridan routed troops under Maj. Gen. George Pickett from this strategic crossroads. His victory caused the evacuation of Petersburg and Richmond and forced the Rebel retreat toward surrender. Stalked by Union troops, Lee's remnant army tried to burn High Bridge, a span over the Appomattox River. Pursuers doused the flames and, scenting imminent capitulation of the foe, dogged him through Virginia woodlands soggy with spring rain.

Faith was about all that Confederate diehards could summon. In late January, Sherman started hacking his way north from Savannah, slashing another wide swath, burning and destroying and tearing the shreds of Rebel morale into fluff as airy as wisps of cotton, preventing precious food and supplies from reaching the emaciated Army of Northern Virginia. Onward he strode, an angel of vengeance to some, a "nightmare, ghoul, hyena" to those in his path. Gamecock Joe Johnston, back in command of the broken Army of Tennessee's remnants and other outfits' shards, was ordered to contest Sherman's advance. He frankly admitted that he could do no more than annoy him.

Sherman was marching again, then, and in front of Petersburg Grant and Lee inspected one another at arm's length, Lee not liking what he saw at all. In the days when the Union policy of attrition gained notoriety, somebody compared the opposing armies to Kilkenny cats which fought until nothing was left but their tails. The story goes that Grant heard this and said, "Our cat has the longer tail."

It was like that now, with a difference. Neither army dared attack frontally; their defenses were too formidable; good soldiers in strong works could not be overwhelmed. Having learned this lesson well at Cold Harbor, Grant was creating attrition by attenuation. When he began branching out around Petersburg, 34,000 Confederates spread themselves thin from above Richmond on down in a 30-mile-long trench system to hold him off. By year-end, a slightly larger Army of Northern Virginia stretched nearly to the breaking point in even longer siege lines. Against it rubbed the 110,000-man Army of the Potomac—and that army's tail curled farther and farther around Petersburg.

Months before, the Union's last head-on try at cracking the lines had blown up in a gory fiasco called the Battle of the Crater. It originated when a number of tough former Pennsylvania coal miners tunneled from Yankee lines more than 500 feet to a point directly beneath a Confederate fort. Then they burrowed 75 feet laterally, in effect crossing the T; perturbed Johnnies 20 feet overhead, hearing strange scraping sounds deep in the earth, probed with shafts of their own but failed to pierce the Yankee mine. The crossbar turned into a sleeping volcano as men carried 320 kegs of black powder into it. An 8,000-pound charge was going to blow the Rebels overhead to Kingdom Come.

As it happened, Ambrose E. Burnside, he of the magnificently whiskered head and the dreadful failure at Fredericksburg in 1862, had a large hand in all this. One of his regimental colonels had seen the mine's possibilities and sold him on it. General Meade okayed the idea; Grant knew about it; Burnside's own men dug the mine and planted the charge; and one of his divisions would spearhead the assault through the blasted Confederate defenses. Petersburg was all but taken.

Three of Burnside's four divisions needed rest badly. The fourth, untested and strong and eager, proudly took on the assignment of leading the assault. These men had personal reason for wanting to perform well. Only a few yesterdays ago they threw off their dreams every morning when the plantation bell rang; these mornings their dreams had form and substance, and the bugle blew Reveille to prove it; they were free men and the only U. S. Colored Troops in the Army of the Potomac. They gladly trained hard to be a worthy spearhead.

At 4:45 a.m. on July 30, 1864, the earth shook and opened and burst heavenward in a flaming, smoke-fogged cataclysm that hurled men sky-high like puppets, tossed cannon aloft as if they were toys, and shredded heavy timbers into flying slivers of death. A Union division moved out to attack—not the Negro troops, however—and immediately ran into trouble; no one had remembered to clear a path through their own defenses. Much worse confusion followed. Incredibly poor leadership, beginning with Burnside, far in the rear, and including the division commander, quaking in a shelter with a bottle of rum, permitted Federals to jam into the mine's vast crater. Another white division piled on, then another, and finally the black soldiers.

At one point thousands of blueclads milled about, and no sitting ducks ever made hunters happier. Rebel infantry charged, artillery smashed down with shell and canister, and black infantrymen died with white. Negro men hadn't led the assault because of a late decision: Grant and Meade didn't want to be accused of trying to sacrifice black troops if the attack failed. Well, nobody *Continued on page 196*

Overleaf: Holocaust illuminates the pell-mell flight of Richmond residents over Mayo's Bridge, April 3. A stubbornly militant Irish woman humiliated departing soldiers with: "Afther fighting them for four years, ye're running like dawgs!"

Gaunt skeletons of Richmond buildings mutely reproach those responsible for the devastating outcome of failure to prepare for orderly evacuation. Fires set hastily by military and civil leaders to destroy Confederate stores encouraged pillagers to use the torch for their own purposes. As mobs waxed riotous, flames consumed more than 700 structures. Distraught and homeless citizens owed much to Union soldiers, who quenched fires and restored order. On April 4, Lincoln went through the streets of the defeated, ruined Capital and heard himself called "Messiah" by rejoicing Negroes. His companion, Admiral Porter, recalled: "I don't think I ever looked upon a scene where there were so many passionately happy faces."

would accuse them of that now; plenty of white men had died first.

It was all over a little after 1 p.m. Ambulatory Federals fled to their lines; the Union's fine opportunity to take Petersburg had fallen apart. Nothing came of it except around 4,000 Northern casualties and a great gash in the earth that you can shake your head at today.

Nothing came of it for the black soldiers either. But they would still serve as a spearhead in a way they themselves didn't comprehend—though they found the words for it welling up in spontaneous song. In evening's gentle hours, the day's soldiering done, they liked to sit around the campfire and sing songs nobody ever heard before because they made them up as they went along. They lifted their voices in music of a sweetness and sadness and depth that white men, listening, could not fathom.

Historian Bruce Catton in his memorable *A Stillness at Appomattox* tells of a new ditty they composed when Burnside gave them the job of leading the attack: "We looks like men a-marching on; We looks like men o'war...." They sang that song on every possible occasion, Mr. Catton observes, until the Battle of the Crater, and then they never chorused it again.

Perhaps they let it go because it ceased to have meaning. When those black soldiers rose up out of the trenches and advanced, cheering, something stirred in them that lives deep in the fiber of humankind. *Look* like men...? No. They were ending all that and, as with all endings, beginning something else. They were moving forward as men. Some evening around the campfire, they would make up a song about it and sing it around all the campfires of their days.

SIEGE WARFARE RESUMED after the Crater, minus Burnside and his rum-swilling commander and some others. They were relieved. The months stretched away; in 100-plus-degree heat soldiers—all sweaty military engineers now—extended their fortifications, and sunstroke leveled some toilers. Dust as fine as pumice puffed up underfoot, coating faces and uniforms and gear, lending food a rusty cast and a grittiness that tormented the teeth. When rain came, mud took over. Heat and flies eased up, but water sometimes stood two feet deep in the trenches. Often the stench of latrines fouled the air and occasionally the choking miasma of unburied bodies drifted in on a transient breeze.

Winter was worst, and far the worst for the Army of Northern Virginia. Snow and sleet caught many men without shoes, as usual, and few wore clothes worthy of the name. Blankets, or what passed for them, looked like greasy rags. Lee's troops were starving. At times they got no meat whatsoever; then they made do with the daily pint of cornmeal. By choice, the general himself fared no better. "Bald Dick" Ewell, commanding at Richmond, once made the mistake of visiting at lunchtime and Lee pressed his meal upon him: two cold sweet potatoes.

Confederate soldiers deserted in droves now, though the penalty was death. Family men often squirmed in an absolutely desperate predicament. Bad enough to look about, shivering and weak, and see no hope; far worse to pore over the latest letter from home: "I don't think if eny thing wod happen you I cod not live long mysef for I can not hardly bare up...." Children sick, winter cruelly cold, clothing in tatters,

Sound of bugles and the beat of drums set the tempo of a Civil War soldier's life. A lad with the New York Engineers carried the drum (right); the bugle halted General Custer's charging cavalry when news came of Lee's surrender. Below, North Carolina schoolteacher Luther Sowers blows assembly for a drill during a celebration of the Civil War Centennial at Fort Fisher.

altogether a hand-to-mouth existence. A man might resolve to go over the hill as soon as darkness fell: ". . . I wod give eny thing if you was home the children and I will pray for you. Your true wife until death Mary."

More stayed on than deserted, however, soldiers as Lee was a soldier, waiting out the end, hoping against hope. People in the North were tired of war; maybe a peace could be negotiated. Or maybe Lee might by some evocation of the old magic give Grant the slip and link up with Johnston down in North Carolina. Lee had this notion in the back of his head. Never say die. Those who would follow him to the death stared across Petersburg's bleak no-man's-land and one summed up their situation like this: "It is a life of sameness & vacancy—Living cannot be called a fever here but rather a long catalepsy."

Bᴜᴛ ᴡᴀʀ ʟᴏᴏᴋs ᴅɪꜰꜰᴇʀᴇɴᴛ to different men; like beauty, it resides in the beholder's eye. For many Federals over at nearby City Point, where the James and Appomattox Rivers join and Grant made his headquarters, the conflict waxed fat and comfortable. There a gigantic supply depot throbbed with vitality; came close, in fact, to choking on its own glut of matériel. Masts of cargo ships stretched away like a forest; 18 trains ran every day carrying the necessities of life and war to the men in the trenches. Nobody in the Union lines suffered from lack of food or warm clothing.

Innumerable citizens made the trip from Washington by paddle-wheeler to goggle at the spectacle. President Lincoln visited too: General Grant and progress reports both were handy. And the General's wife and their four children lived at City Point at various times during the war's last months. Call U. S. Grant a great, tough, and single-minded soldier; call him a gentle and loving family man too, which is a side of him few of us have seen.

Early in February three emissaries from Jefferson Davis passed through the lines—Yanks and Rebs standing on the parapets to cheer them—and conferred with Lincoln and Seward aboard the steamer *River Queen* in Hampton Roads. They sought peace terms, as Davis enjoined them, for "the two countries." Lincoln could only see one country, and that was that. Back to work went the armies.

President Davis discussed the peace mission in a fiery speech on February 6, reportedly denouncing Lincoln as "His Majesty Abraham the First," and adding that before the campaign was over he and Seward might find "they had been speaking to their masters."

Politicians rave; soldiers learn the truth. Within 48 hours, Robert E. Lee informed Secretary of War Seddon that some of his men "had been without meat for three days, and all were . . . exposed to battle, cold, hail, and sleet." Lee pulled no punches. ". . . I apprehend dire results. The physical strength of the men, if their courage survives, must fail under this treatment. . . . Taking these facts in connection with the paucity of our numbers, you must not be surprised if calamity befalls us."

Grant didn't think that Lee could hold on much longer either; when the winter-bogged roads dried and the Army of the Potomac moved out in the spring campaign, the war would end. Only one possibility bothered the Union commander: Lee might slip away one night, to go south for new battles. The war might be prolonged another year.

Calamity engulfs the South, but hoping against hope, Rebel soldiers in Gilbert Gaul's allegorical painting fight desperately from "The Confederate Raft" beside their leader and their flag. For a month after the defeat of Lee and Johnston's armies, a few Southerners continued to fight for their lost cause.

GILBERT GAUL, C. 1875, N. S. MEYER, INC.

Three men, three viewpoints: Davis promising his people great successes, if they cooperated; Lee watching his once-magnificent army disintegrate and finding the face of disaster behind it; Grant pacing impatiently, cigar clamped in mouth, anxious to get the whole miserable business over with.

There was a fourth viewpoint, far broader and more profound than the others. It belonged to Abraham Lincoln and it amounted to a vision. On March 4, at the United States Capitol, the President rose beneath drizzly skies to deliver his Second Inaugural Address. A lonely man among the multitude, he advanced to the table, and the sun burst forth.

Wearing a new dress uniform, Lee accepts surrender terms in the parlor of Wilmer McLean's home at Appomattox Court House. Beside him stands his secretary, Lt. Col. Charles Marshall. In muddy boots and rumpled fatigue blouse bearing three-star shoulder straps, Grant watches compassionately. His companions include Sheridan, Col. Orville E. Babcock, Lt. Col. Horace Porter, Maj. Gen. Edward O. C. Ord, Maj. Gen. Seth Williams, Col. Theodore S. Bowers, Col. Ely S. Parker, and Maj. Gen. George A. Custer. Later, Marshall paid tribute to Grant's liberal terms: "As far as it was possible, General Grant took away the sting of defeat from the Confederate Army. He triumphed . . . without exultation, and with a noble respect to his enemy." But Lee's veterans wept for their vanquished leader and, for the last time (right), tenderly furled their flags — shrouds for dead hopes.

TOM LOVELL (ABOVE); RICHARD NORRIS BROOKE, 1872, WEST POINT MUSEUM, ALEXANDER McCOOK CRAIGHEAD COLLECTION

With his son Maj. Gen. G. W. C. Lee (left) and his aide Col. Walter Taylor, Lee reluctantly poses for a Brady portrait in Richmond eight days after surrender. Drawn face and brooding eyes bespeak the defeated hero's anguish. A month later, Grant's protection saved Lee from arrest and trial for treason.

It flooded the great crowded plaza, golden omen, setting hearts aglow.

Then Lincoln shaped his vision, his theology, into words that soar and inspire perhaps even more in our discordant day than they did then: "With malice toward none; with charity for all; with firmness in the right, as God gives us to see the right. . . ." The long night's journey into day was ending; the President anticipated the dawn.

S HERMAN ADVANCED into North Carolina, inflexible in the right as he saw it. Joe Johnston planned to attack a wing of his army, near the village of Bentonville. On March 19 Johnston's makeshift army swept forward yelling beneath its faded flags and drove the Federals from the field for one final lightning flash of victory. Its brief light proved that nothing could keep Sherman's 90,000 men from their appointment with Grant. Six days later Robert E. Lee tried and failed to break past Fort Stedman at Petersburg, a last-gasp effort to cut his way out and team up with Johnston farther south. It was almost over.

As April arrived, hard-driving Phil Sheridan crashed into game Confederates anchoring the Army of Northern Virginia's right flank at the junction of Five Forks. When George Pickett's men crumbled there (Pickett himself had gone to a shad bake in the rear), U. S. Grant finally outflanked Lee, readying the noose. Thousands of Union soldiers had died trying for nearly a year to accomplish this, and untold thousands of Southerners had died trying to prevent it.

They were all Americans to Lincoln. As he said, he had been living a horrid dream for four years. With Lee forced to telegraph Davis that Petersburg and Richmond must be abandoned, Lincoln's nightmare vanished in the flaming hell that consumed the Rebel Capital. While drunken mobs pillaged and Richmond burned, Davis and his Cabinet rode a train 135 miles southwest to Danville, and Lee's scarecrow army retreated in the same direction. Somewhere, Davis aimed to re-establish his government; somewhere, Lee hoped to defend it.

Lincoln entered the smoldering city on April 4, greatly embarrassed when Negroes fell on their knees before him. He made them rise: "You must kneel to God only." Walking on, fanning himself that warm morning with his stovepipe hat, he paused at notorious Libby Prison; it had penned more than 1,000 Union officers in eight rooms. "Leave it as a monument," he said. Proceeding to the Confederate White House, already serving as Federal headquarters, he lunched there. Touring its high-style Victorian rooms, he sat for a spell at Jefferson Davis's desk. In the afternoon, tired out, he returned to his waiting ship, wanting its quiet. His remaining days numbered ten.

And the war ran down swiftly to the finish. Lee's exhausted veterans, thousands deserting, trudged westward on empty bellies to escape; Grant's ebullient Yanks, tasting victory, drove hard to get around them; both armies plodded ever nearer a peaceful county seat with a poetic Indian name: Appomattox. A mere 140 or so miles south, at Goldsboro, Sherman was readying for the final thrust into Virginia.

On April 7 Grant knew Lee's position was hopeless. "I . . . regard it as my duty," he wrote, "to shift from myself the responsibility of any further effusion of blood, by asking of you the surrender of that portion of the Confederate States army known as the Army of Northern Virginia."

Two days later, on Palm Sunday, Lee conceded. Truce flags fluttered while the armies rested on the greening swell of the farmland around Appomattox Court House and their commanders met in the parlor of Wilmer McLean's brick home. McLean may have been the world's most astounded man. The hard fighting had begun back in '61 by storming across his yard at Bull Run, and he moved away so it wouldn't happen

In the McLean parlor, Robbie Jordan questions the author about a copy of Grant's surrender terms. Reproductions replace original tables and chairs now in museums. After the signing, contents of the room were bought or carried away as mementos of the historic occasion.

again, and now the whole thing was winding up in his living room.

Lee the patrician wore his fine dress uniform and sword to the meeting. Grant the plain man attended in working clothes—muddy boots and a fatigue blouse with three stars on the shoulder straps—and swordless. Here they sat, two sons of America as disparate as the North and South they represented. Yet what they produced in this small, sedate room proved the greatest triumph of either, for they closed the war with honor for all, without rancor or exultation, with magnanimity and respect by the one and wisdom and courage by the other.

As one who has followed U. S. Grant's career at considerable length, I believe that this was his finest hour. Having taken away, he gave back in fullest measure. He achieved the beginning of reconciliation for the Nation—would that later measures had been so wise and compassionate!—with marvelously simple terms.

Grant had it all in mind; he now put it on paper. Officers and men of the Army of Northern Virginia would give their paroles. They would hand over arms, artillery, and public property. Officers could keep their horses and side arms (and Robert Louis Stevenson would write that it was a great gentleman who had no desire to take Lee's sword). This done, everyone could go home; they would not be disturbed by United States authority while they observed their paroles and the laws where they lived. So saying, Grant guaranteed in one sentence that no treason trials would keep old wounds festering, and none did.

Lee liked the terms. They would, he said, have a happy effect on his army. There *was* one thing: Many of his cavalrymen and artillerists owned their own horses—could they keep them?

"I think we have fought the last battle of the war," Grant replied; "...it is doubtful whether they will be able to put in a crop to carry themselves and their families through the next winter without the aid of the horses they are now riding." Yes, every man who claimed to own a horse or mule could take the animal home.

There it was. Time had run out. The war was over. So Grant thought; so most of us think today. Something like 150,000 of us tour Appomattox Court House National Historical Park every year, poking in the old general store, fancying that a stagecoach is pulling up to Clover Hill Tavern. Traipsing through the reconstructed McLean House, we sense the immensity of what happened in this rural village.

The war did end here, and yet one more great infantry battle was raging. A couple of hours after Grant and Lee finished their work it rose to a last high drama at Blakeley, Alabama, a town on the lines guarding the eastern approach to Mobile. Some 16,000 Federals stepped off smartly in line of battle, charging like Pickett at Gettysburg and Grant at Cold Harbor and Hood at Franklin. Advancing over a 2½-mile front, they marched across bursting land mines and hacked their way through felled trees and telegraph-wire obstacles, receiving heavy musketry and

John Wilkes Booth fires the fatal shot at Lincoln, whose wife and young friends watch a play at Ford's Theatre in Washington, D. C., on April 14, 1865. Borne to a house across the street, the suffering President endured until 7:22 next morning, when the doctor announced, "He is gone." Booth, trapped by pursuers in a Virginia barn 11 days later, died from gunshot wounds shortly after his capture.

artillery fire the while. The whole thing lasted about 20 minutes, ending when they overwhelmed the defending Rebels—a leavening of experienced troops, old men, and a brigade of boy reserves.

The records do not tell us, of course, how many boys lay among the dead. More than 3,400 prisoners were rounded up, however. Some were forced to locate, cap, and dig up the unexploded land mines—it was that or be marched back and forth in a body until all had blown up.

It served no real purpose, this fight, like many others, and few today realize it occurred. B. L. Roberson of Mobile, an authority on Alabama's part in the war, took me to the little-known battleground. A jungle now, it rests in peace as anonymously as the thousands and tens of thousands of nameless grave markers that dot Civil War cemeteries. Live oaks tower over the field and pine needles carpet the old trenches and even the village itself—once it was larger than Mobile—has disappeared almost without trace.

BLAKELEY RANKS HIGH among the war's caprices. Fort Sumter stands alone. Here in Charleston Harbor the hostilities began. On April 14, 1861, Maj. Robert Anderson hauled Old Glory down, surrendered the fort to the Confederacy, and steamed north with his garrison. Here, on April 14, 1865, retired Maj. Gen. Robert Anderson raised the same flag over Fort Sumter that he had lowered four years earlier to the day.

It was a great day, and Henry Ward Beecher made a stirring speech. It was Good Friday, too. Up at Raleigh, North Carolina, General Sherman received a message from his old adversary General Johnston proposing that the two of them take steps toward peace. But that evening in Washington, as President Lincoln watched a comedy at Ford's Theatre, the assassin John Wilkes Booth put a pistol bullet in the President's head, and the great day turned to ashes.

Word of Lincoln's death spread slowly in some areas. Sherman learned of it only on the morning of the 17th while leaving to arrange Johnston's surrender. He met the Rebel commander at the Bennett place, a small farmhouse near Durham, and in private showed him the dispatch announcing the President's assassination. In his reaction, the Confederate general mirrored, I believe, the horror and concern felt by all thinking Southerners. "The perspiration came out in large drops on his forehead," Sherman observed, "and he did not attempt to conceal his distress." Johnston maintained that the loss was most serious to the South, whose people "had begun to realize that Mr. Lincoln was the best friend they had."

To memorialize their meeting, North Carolina has designated the Bennett place a State Historic Site, and a reconstructed dwelling stands there. Near it rises a simple yet imposing monument, gray marble. I found the living legacy of Sherman and Johnston elsewhere, however —in Southerners like my friend Mary Ann Harrell who grew up not too far away. Mary Ann points out that the monument's twin columns rest on a north-south axis. And then she looks at the beam overhead that ties the columns together. One word is carved in it: UNITY.

How sad that Jefferson Davis could not abide this word. On May 10, deep in Georgia, still fleeing, he was captured near Irwinville by a detachment of the 4th Michigan Cavalry. With him in custody, the

Grieving citizens view their martyred President's body at City Hall in New York. After the official funeral in Washington, Lincoln lay in state in 11 cities along the train route to his final resting place. On May 4 he was entombed in Oak Ridge Cemetery in Springfield, Illinois, with Willie, the son whose death he had mourned in 1862.

HARPER'S WEEKLY, 1865

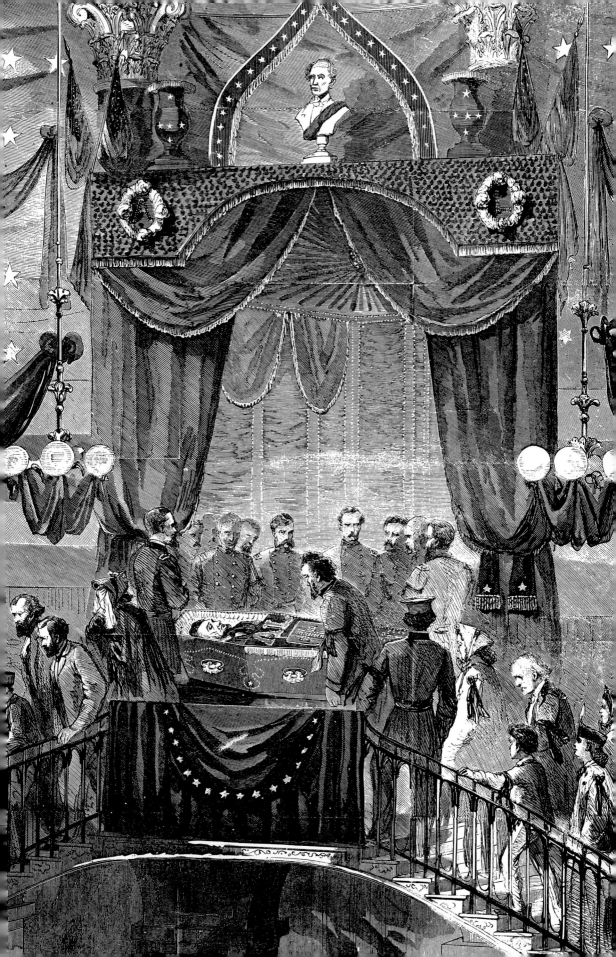

Blue billow of Army of the Potomac veterans passes the White House reviewing stand during the Grand Review, May 23. Bright red-white-and-blue bunting replaced mourning crape as Wash-

*ington honored its victorious defenders. Next day, Sherman led his army along the same crowd-
thronged route. More than a third of a million Union soldiers had perished before this final parade.* 209

Confederate Government ceased to be. The last skirmish occurred three days later near Brownsville, Texas, and, on May 26, Confederate forces in the trans-Mississippi surrendered.

The Confederate President was imprisoned at Fort Monroe. Accused of plotting Lincoln's assassination, he suffered the indignity of being shackled briefly. It was cruel humiliation for the proud man, and he put up a stiff fight until his jailers subdued him.

I DROVE MY FAMILY one day to Fort Monroe and we talked of what happened to some of the people we have come to know. General Grant—"one of those still plain men that do the world's rough work," as James Russell Lowell wrote—moved on to the White House in 1869. Simon B. Buckner, who unhappily submitted at Fort Donelson to Grant's demand for unconditional surrender, served as a pallbearer at Grant's funeral in 1885; two years later Buckner became Governor of Kentucky. George McClellan served as Governor of New Jersey (1878-81).

Robert E. Lee accepted the presidency of Washington College (now Washington and Lee University). He died, 63 years old and worn out, in 1870. Jefferson Davis one day would hail him as "the deathless martyr of our kingdom of the twilight."

My wife, descendant of Southerners, had sympathized with the luckless civilians caught in Sherman's devastating marches—as did that general himself, to a degree. "How," Jane asked, "did Sherman's life turn out?" Pretty much as you might expect, I replied. Sherman succeeded Grant as General-in-Chief. Retiring in 1884, he was regarded as a prime presidential prospect; he dismissed such talk in a famous sentence: "I will not accept if nominated, and will not serve if elected." Sherman died in 1891; his enemy of old, General Johnston, postwar businessman and Member of Congress, insisted on standing hatless in

Against a mist-draped sun a bronze bugler and his comrade stand eternally tensed fo

the cold at his funeral. Weakened and ill, Johnston died a month later.

My son Robbie recalled a Rebel colonel who rode along the lines at Champion Hill, holding reins and a magnolia flower in one hand and sword in the other, crying his men forward. "Did he live?" my boy asked. He did. Francis M. Cockrell—captured at Blakeley—became a Senator from Missouri and Chairman of the Interstate Commerce Commission.

I didn't tell Rob what happened to another gallant Southerner—he can read it here—who carried water to wounded and dying Northerners after the slaughter at Fredericksburg. Young Sgt. Richard Kirkland was killed at Chickamauga.

And what of Jeff Davis? We spent an hour in the cell he occupied at Fort Monroe, with daylight seeping through a single small window. Reading the Bible, the prisoner could hear his guards speculating: "Do you think they'll hang him. . . ?" I peered through the grated embrasure just as Davis had done, sad for this courageous man. He could only look south, south at the land he loved and lost. Gulls wheeled above the moat's green water as I paused there, relieving the oppression; did they do as much for the Confederacy's President?

Becoming quite ill, he was transferred to better quarters at the fort. On May 13, 1867, he was released on $100,000 bail, and in 1869 the charges against him were dropped. He died 20 years later, 81 years old and unreconstructed to the end.

But the year before he died he made a little speech in Mississippi to a group of young men. It seems to me an appropriate way to close this account, and his, for in it he showed that at last he too had accepted the idea of union and the United States: "Let me beseech you," said Jefferson Davis, "to lay aside all rancor, all bitter sectional feeling, and to make your places in the ranks of those who will bring about a consummation devoutly to be wished—a reunited country."

battle at the base of the Virginia Monument at Gettysburg. Across these fields, Pickett had led his ill-fated charge.
VOLKMAR WENTZEL, NATIONAL GEOGRAPHIC STAFF

INDEX

Illustrations references appear in *italics*.

Additional References

For additional reading, you may wish to refer to the following NATIONAL GEOGRAPHIC articles and to check the Cumulative Index for related material: Lonnelle Aikman, "New Stars for Old Glory," July 1959; Robert T. Cochran, Jr., "Witness to a War: British Correspondent Frank Vizetelly," April 1961; William S. Ellis, "Atlanta, Pacesetter City of the South," Feb. 1969; Ulysses S. Grant 3rd, Major General, USA (Ret.), "Appomattox: Where Grant and Lee Made Peace With Honor a Century Ago," April 1965; and "The Civil War," April 1961; William Graves, "Mobile, Alabama's City in Motion," March 1968; Robert Paul Jordan, "Gettysburg and Vicksburg: the Battle Towns Today," July 1963; John and Blanche Leeper, "American Processional: History on Canvas," Feb. 1951; Carolyn Bennett Patterson, "Our Land Through Lincoln's Eyes," Feb. 1960; Carl Sandburg, "Just a Hundred Years Ago," July 1963; and "Lincoln, Man of Steel and Velvet," Feb. 1960; Volkmar Wentzel, "History Awakens at Harpers Ferry," March 1957; "Battlefields Map Traces a Nation's Conflict," April 1961.

You may wish to refer to the following books produced by the National Geographic Society:

America's Historylands, 1967; *America's Wonderlands*, 1966; *Equal Justice Under Law*, 1965; *Our Country's Presidents*, 1969; *The Living White House*, 1967; *The White House*, 1969; and *We, the People*, 1969.

Composition for The Civil War by National Geographic's Phototypographic Division. Color separations by Beck Engraving Co., Philadelphia, Pa.; R. R. Donnelley & Sons, Inc., Chicago, Ill.; Graphic Color Plate Inc., Stamford, Conn.; The Lanman Co., Alexandria, Va.; and Progressive Color Corp., Rockville, Md. This edition printed by Kingsport Press, Kingsport, Tenn.

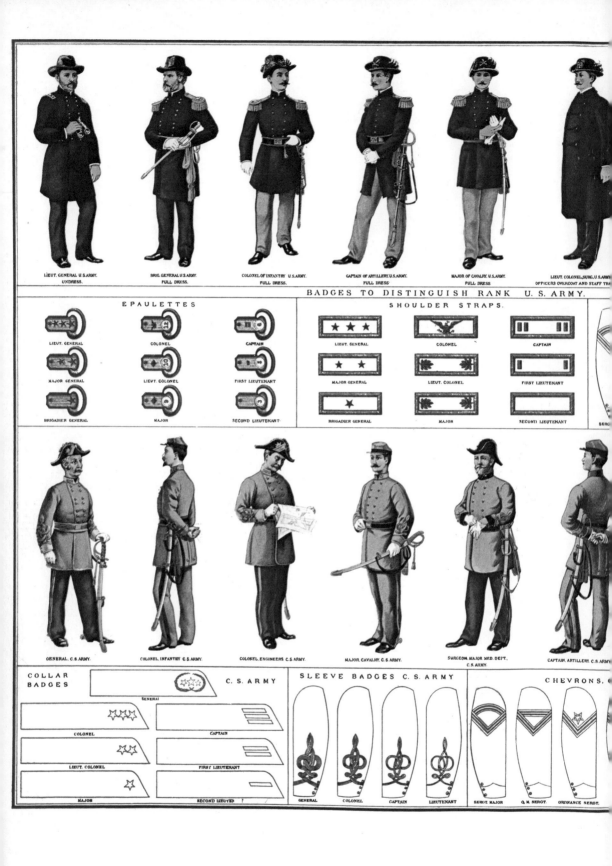

LIEUT. GENERAL. U.S.ARMY. UNDRESS.

BRIG. GENERAL U.S.ARMY. FULL DRESS.

COLONEL OF INFANTRY U.S.ARMY. FULL DRESS.

CAPTAIN OF ARTILLERY. U.S.ARMY. FULL DRESS.

MAJOR OF CAVALRY. U.S.ARMY. FULL DRESS.

LIEUT. COLONEL, SURG. U.S.ARMY. OFFICERS OVERCOAT AND STAFF TRA

BADGES TO DISTINGUISH RANK   U.S. ARMY.

EPAULETTES

LIEUT. GENERAL

MAJOR GENERAL

BRIGADIER GENERAL

COLONEL

LIEUT. COLONEL

MAJOR

CAPTAIN

FIRST LIEUTENANT

SECOND LIEUTENANT

SHOULDER STRAPS.

LIEUT. GENERAL

MAJOR GENERAL

BRIGADIER GENERAL

COLONEL

LIEUT. COLONEL

MAJOR

CAPTAIN

FIRST LIEUTENANT

SECOND LIEUTENANT

SERG

GENERAL, C.S. ARMY.

COLONEL, INFANTRY C.S.ARMY.

COLONEL, ENGINEERS C.S.ARMY.

MAJOR, CAVALRY. C.S. ARMY.

SURGEON, MAJOR MED. DEP'T, C.S. ARMY.

CAPTAIN, ARTILLERY, C.S. ARMY

COLLAR BADGES

C. S. ARMY

GENERAL

COLONEL

LIEUT. COLONEL

MAJOR

CAPTAIN

FIRST LIEUTENANT

SECOND LIEUTEN ?

SLEEVE BADGES C.S. ARMY

GENERAL

COLONEL

CAPTAIN

LIEUTENANT

CHEVRONS,

SERGT MAJOR

Q. M. SERGT.

ORDNANCE SERGT.